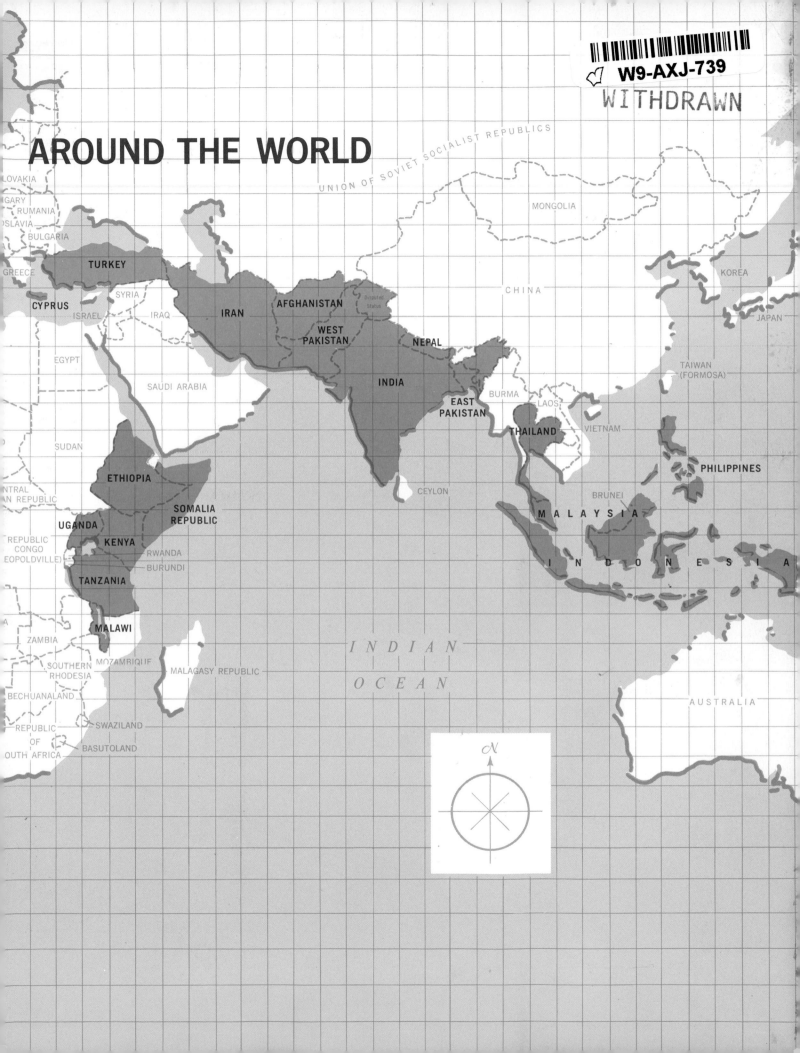

AROUND THE WORLD

UNION OF SOVIET SOCIALIST REPUBLICS

LOVAKIA
GARY
RUMANIA
OSLAVIA
BULGARIA
GREECE

MONGOLIA

KOREA

TURKEY

CHINA

JAPAN

CYPRUS
SYRIA
ISRAEL
IRAQ
IRAN
AFGHANISTAN
Disputed Status
WEST PAKISTAN
NEPAL

TAIWAN (FORMOSA)

EGYPT

SAUDI ARABIA

INDIA

EAST PAKISTAN

BURMA
LAOS
VIETNAM

SUDAN

THAILAND

PHILIPPINES

CEYLON

BRUNEI

ETHIOPIA

MALAYSIA

NTRAL
AN REPUBLIC

SOMALIA REPUBLIC

UGANDA
REPUBLIC CONGO
EOPOLDVILLE)
KENYA
RWANDA
BURUNDI

INDONESIA

TANZANIA

MALAWI
ZAMBIA
SOUTHERN RHODESIA
MOZAMBIQUE
MALAGASY REPUBLIC

INDIAN

OCEAN

BECHUANALAND

AUSTRALIA

REPUBLIC OF OUTH AFRICA
SWAZILAND
BASUTOLAND

N

WITHDRAWN

The Peace Corps

This is new, and it is also very old. We have in a sense come full circle. We have come from the tyranny of the enormous, awesome, discordant machine, back to the realization that the beginning and the end are man—that it is man who is important, not the machine, and that it is man who accounts for growth, not just dollars or factories. Above all, that it is man who is the object of all our efforts.

Pablo Casals

The
Peace Corps

A Pictorial History

Edited by Aaron J. Ezickson

Introduction by Sargent Shriver

ⱴ Hill and Wang, New York

Acknowledgment

The editor and publisher owe a great debt to the Peace Corps, which by opening its photographic files and by providing information otherwise unobtainable made this book possible.

Contents

The Road to Peace

Sargent Shriver

The road to peace is no highway.

It is racked with wars, riddled with mistrust and suspicion. Ruts and potholes of poverty and ignorance are deep enough to bring Atlas to his knees. If humanity ever hopes to pave this road it must accomplish an understanding deeper and more durable than the world has ever known.

The search for this understanding has begun. The people of many nations are sharing in it. In the full panorama of this great quest, the Peace Corps plays only a small part. And yet the Peace Corps is there— in the heart of the most important struggle of our times. That is what matters, whether the role of the Peace Corps is small or large. Sometimes even the smallest program will set up ripples that reach unbelievable distances.

St. Lucia, an island in the Caribbean, was one of the first places in the world to ask for Peace Corps Volunteers. I visited the Volunteers there shortly after they went to work. I am not inclined to misgivings, but I couldn't help thinking: There are so few of them—and their assignment is so large. How can they ever accomplish anything?

Some people have asked this question about the entire Peace Corps. Volunteers are working in nations whose populations add up to almost 900,000,-000. A mere ten thousand Volunteers were at work on March 1, 1965, the fourth birthday of the Peace Corps. Doesn't it seem likely that even a hundred thousand Volunteers would vanish, swallowed up by sheer multitudes?

Perhaps the question can be answered on St. Lucia.

Fragments of an answer took the form of three precious eggs and a postage stamp. I first heard about the postage stamp in December, 1964. The government of St. Lucia announced its intention then to issue a stamp honoring the Volunteers who had served there. This stamp, a remarkable tribute to the Peace Corps, says a great deal about Volunteer effectiveness. There were never more than fifteen Volunteers on St. Lucia at any one time.

Malinda DuBose (Miami, Fla.), a nurse and a member of the first group to arrive on the island, described what being there meant to her: "These experiences will come to you in ways that cannot be described in words, but perhaps you will recognize their worth the first time a child comes to you after a clinic and says, 'These are for you.' You look into the small bag he is holding out to you and there are three precious eggs from his home. He smiles, and you know he is saying, 'Thank you'. . . ."

These eggs are a tribute as impressive in their way as the postage stamp. The Volunteers on St. Lucia, few as they were, quickly put themselves "on first-name terms with thousands," as the island's leading newspaper reported. The newspaper, the *Voice of St. Lucia*, went on to indicate that Volunteer friendliness stood in marked contrast to the attitude of many previous visitors to the island. These visitors, the article said, might even be "shocked" by it.

Volunteers have been generating "shocks" like this all over the world. The voltage generated by simple friendliness is part of the measure of Volunteer effectiveness in forty-six nations of Asia, Africa, and Latin America. Each day supplies new evidence that Peace Corps Volunteers are the best bearers of good will that this nation—perhaps any nation—ever sent beyond its borders.

This is not to say that the Peace Corps hasn't had its problems. Slightly more than 8 per cent of all Volunteers have had to return home before their two years of service were completed. Some early returns were due to unavoidable circumstances—a death in the family, a medical problem. Others, about half of them, returned early because the Volunteers couldn't take it or they came to dislike the Peace Corps or they decided they would never accomplish anything.

Each Volunteer who goes overseas has been asked for by someone in the host country. Even so, the Volunteer's prospective job sometimes turns out to be a mirage. When this happens, the Peace Corps must see to it that the Volunteer gets a full-time job as soon as possible. His morale is quickly shattered if he becomes convinced he isn't needed. On a few occasions, unemployed Volunteers have quit and gone home before a job was found for them. In one instance, the Volunteer didn't even wait to see if he had a proper job. He took one look around the airport and grabbed the next plane for home.

All but a few Volunteers find substantial, full-time jobs waiting for them at the other end of the long overseas flight. They have been asked for, and they are put to work, in response to the needs of the age we live in.

St. Lucia's Chief Minister, John G. M. Compton, expressed that idea in a speech in late 1964. The occasion was the turnover by the United States of a former American military base on St. Lucia to the island's government. "The close of an era does not make the end of our relationship—rather the opening of a wider association altered to meet the needs and temper of our time," Compton said. "The soldiers' barracks have given way to a new high school to be named the John F. Kennedy Memorial High School. The drill sergeant's bark has yielded to the persuasive drawl of the U. S. Peace Corps Volunteers. . . ."

The Peace Corps was born by an Executive Order of the President. John F. Kennedy brought it into existence on March 1, 1961. Not quite seven months later, Congress gave the new organization its stamp of approval by passing the Peace Corps Bill. This bill appropriated $32 million to run the Peace Corps in its first full fiscal year, July 1, 1961, to June 30, 1962. It also established three goals for the new agency: (1) to help the people of developing nations meet their needs for trained manpower; (2) to help promote a better understanding of the American people on the part of the peoples served; and (3) to help promote a better understanding of other peoples on the part of the American people.

How is the Peace Corps fulfilling these three goals? Take them in reverse order and consider the third goal first.

The Peace Corps seeks to offer a new awareness of the world not only to Volunteers but to every American interested in "the needs and temper of our times." The quality of this new awareness, its impact on our society, will become increasingly evident as

Volunteers return from Peace Corps service in ever greater numbers. One small but interesting effect was visible before the Peace Corps was three years old. It concerned the Peace Corps' own training programs.

Every Volunteer who goes overseas first completes a training program. Training usually lasts twelve weeks. The curriculum includes, among other courses, a study of the customs, culture, and history of the countries for which the trainees are bound. When the Peace Corps was new, training programs sometimes found no one at all capable of teaching these courses. This is not to say that no Americans were capable of teaching them. But with regard to some of the countries to which Volunteers were going, this whole nation could only produce ten or twelve experts. If all of them happened to be tied up, the Peace Corps was out of luck.

This is a problem no longer. The Peace Corps has generated its own supply of experts—the returned Peace Corps Volunteers. In the case of one particular country, we now have, in addition to the few men who were once the sole American experts, more than a hundred Volunteers who have served there for two years and returned home, who speak the language and know the customs. When it came time to train fresh groups for this country, the Peace Corps was readily able to contract with these former Volunteers to teach the necessary culture, geography, economics, and history courses. In many ways, from the Peace Corps point of view, they make better teachers than outside experts because they are aware of the specific problems that Volunteers will face.

Now for the second goal of the Peace Corps as laid down by Congress. The openness, the friendliness, the spirit of Volunteers have revolutionized local attitudes toward Americans all over the world. The cry, "Yankee, go home," is being replaced around the world by the request, "Send us more Peace Corps Volunteers." Sometimes, the very people who have shouted, "Yankee, go home," have been the same ones to ask for more Volunteers.

The Volunteers have accomplished this change. Best of all, they have done it without conscious design. They have not set out on a public relations campaign to win the affections of others. The idea of such a campaign is anathema to them. But they have won the affections of others all the same. They have done it with the revolutionary technique of confronting their overseas neighbors with a minimum of sham and pretense. They have appeared in overseas neighborhoods as persons who genuinely want to help others, as human beings, one to another.

Some might object to the term "revolutionary." I don't mean to say that Volunteers invented the idea of behaving naturally in an overseas setting. They are certainly not the first attractive persons to sail off to work in other parts of the world either as individuals or as members of remarkable organizations. The revolutionary part of the Peace Corps approach lies in the scale on which it is being applied. And certainly government as such has never before sent representatives overseas burdened with no protocol or official orders other than the instructions to work hard and "be yourself."

And because Volunteers are themselves, they are able to work at the grass roots. In this sense, the second goal of the Peace Corps is inseparable from the first.

St. Lucia will issue a Peace Corps postage stamp only partly because St. Lucians like the Volunteers. I am sure that Volunteers are being honored most of all for the work they have done, for what they have accomplished in St. Lucia in agriculture, education, and public health. And yet they would probably have accomplished much less if they had not been the kind of people they are. Like Volunteers everywhere, they came prepared to live in a certain way— on the same economic level as their hosts. They had to bring sympathy and special insights to their assigned tasks. They had to be the kind of people who want to live and work where the Peace Corps works —in urban slums, in remote villages, sometimes in overseas universities, but more often among the dispossessed.

I have never ceased to be amazed at how many "soft, spoiled, and overrich" Americans want this kind of life. In its first four years, the Peace Corps received more than 135,000 applications.

In four years, also, the Volunteers racked up enough accomplishments, in the usual sense of the term, to fill a fat volume. In that time, they taught literally millions of hours of classes. They fed hundreds of thousands of children in school lunch programs. They stimulated self-help programs in thousands of remote villages. They organized programs in the slums of most of the major cities of Latin America. They reformed agricultural practices, built schools, helped modernize hospitals, organized country clinics. They conducted surveys and geological expeditions, codified laws, organized cooperatives, and found markets for the works of craftsmen where none before existed. They even assisted countries at the birth of nationwide educational television systems.

I could go on and on. But at the Peace Corps we have never measured Volunteer accomplishment solely by a list of this kind. We have felt that the Volunteers' profoundest accomplishments—their true fulfillment of the Peace Corps' number one goal—have been results more difficult to measure.

Much of the world stands poised at the foot of a ladder, ready and eager to start the climb. To other parts of it the message must be brought: that people can help themselves, that they can improve their lives by their own efforts. Among those who are bringing this message are Peace Corps Volunteers, but they must pass the word on softly, so as not to disrupt the lives of their listeners, so as not to alienate them. They must join them in their daily lives. And when they do that, Volunteers find that their own lives become altered, that their attitudes are changed beyond all recognition.

In some parts of the world, educational systems put a premium on memorizing. The Volunteer who encounters such systems often realizes for the first time that he himself has a wholly different view of the purpose of education: he thinks education should produce men who can reason for themselves. He becomes conscious of his assumptions in the act of using them in his classrooms. Perhaps he changes a few attitudes and convinces some of his students of the paramount value of reason and imagination. In any case, he finds his own values modified and sharpened by the teaching experience.

And he is a good teacher. Within a few years of his arrival overseas, his students are passing examinations in significantly larger numbers than ever before.

Changes in attitudes can be measured with scientific polling techniques. If such polls are taken in the developing world, they will probably not be directed toward attitudes relevant to the Peace Corps. Will polls ever measure the growing awareness of the value of self-help? Yet in the long haul, this is where the work of the Peace Corps will be of profoundest importance.

The first Volunteers to join the Peace Corps were repeatedly asked one question over and over: Why did you join? They quickly learned to resent the question. To some of them, it seemed to imply another question: Aren't you a little crazy to walk out on air conditioning, automobiles, hot and cold running water? Many Volunteers didn't know why they had joined. Others found their reasons too personal to put into words, or at least to tell to strangers.

The fact is that the thirteen thousand men and women who have served, or are serving, in the Peace Corps have had many reasons for joining. Most joined not for one reason but for several, some selfish and some distinctly unselfish. Some joined out of a genuine desire to help others. But who could confess to that without sounding like a stuffed shirt?

You can see this when you talk with them. As individuals, Volunteers are involved in the problems of our times. They have decided to participate in the great struggle of our times—the fight against ignorance, misery, and despair. This involvement, more than anything else, unites the Volunteers. It lies at the heart of the Volunteer point of view, if you can say there is such a thing among so many diverse people. Volunteers come from all fifty states plus the District of Columbia, Puerto Rico, and Guam. Their ranks include Ph.D.'s as well as a few who never finished high school. The Peace Corps has welcomed them all, sophisticated "city slickers" and farm boys from the Dakotas, and all those in between ranging in age from eighteen to seventy-nine.

David Ziegenhagen (Hopkins, Minn.) was a member of the first group of Volunteers to go to the Philippines. In his second year there, he was sent to northern Luzon to help lay the groundwork for a fresh group of Volunteers who were about to be assigned to the mountainous rice-terrace country above Lingayen Gulf. Even then, people were still asking Ziegenhagen why he had joined the Peace Corps. One day he replied, "I am happy to say that I still cannot answer that question. Whatever my original motivation was, it has long since been pushed aside by the Peace Corps experience itself, and not even hindsight can recover it. Every day, I discover at least a dozen reasons why I should have volunteered."

The Peace Corps will one day be administered largely by former Volunteers. Ziegenhagen was one of the first of them to be asked to join the staff. He accepted and was assigned to Thailand, where he is helping to direct one of the Peace Corps' most interesting new programs: an effort to erase malaria from the nation.

This program evolved out of a series of talks between the Thai Ministry of Health and John McCarthy, Peace Corps Representative in Thailand. It was developed partly on the basis of researches carried out by three of the first Volunteers to go to Thailand, members of a group which arrived in January, 1962. The program quickly gained the co-operation of the United States Agency for International Development and the World Health Organization. It now employs fourteen Volunteers, public health experts, who are assigned as administrators in fourteen of the antimalaria "zones" into which Thailand is divided.

Malaria eradication, as such, is not new in the world. It might seem at first glance to demand only the high-level technical direction through which such programs have been administered in the past. As a result of the Thailand program, we now know that malaria eradication can be adapted to the Peace Corps way of doing things and still lose none of its effectiveness; indeed, a few bonuses result from bringing Volunteers into the attack. This kind of exploration looks over known territories with a new perspective.

On September 20, 1963, Colombia welcomed forty-one Volunteers whose arrival touched off an experiment made possible by a technological triumph. Radiotelevisora Nacional, the most highly developed television system in Latin America, was capable of reaching 85 per cent of Colombia's population and 94 per cent of its elementary schools. These figures were especially remarkable in a country containing three ranges of the colossal Andes, which make the nation a collection of blind valleys rimmed by immense mountains. In contrast to the advanced state of Colombian television were the nation's rural schools, many of which were trying to function without textbooks or equipment of any kind. Their teachers often had no more than a fifth-grade education. By Colombian estimate, half the nation was illiterate.

It was a brilliant idea, then, to use the technological advance in one field to counter the lag in the other. Educational television, broadcast on channels available to Radiotelevisora Nacional, could beam into almost every school a flow of material far beyond the resources of any single school. The Alliance for Progress thought enough of the idea to supply fifteen hundred television sets to be placed in schools and communities throughout Colombia. Essential to the experiment in all its aspects would be Peace Corps Volunteers.

Many of the first forty-one Volunteers to join this fascinating program remained in the city of Bogotá. There they worked out the basic structure of educational programming, wrote scripts, gathered educational materials, and directed the separate sequences, working closely throughout with Colombian colleagues. Other Volunteers went to the provinces, where they began a campaign of instructing school and community authorities in the technique of getting the most out of the television programs that would soon be coming their way. After almost two years, much still remained to be done and the first group was augmented by fresh Volunteers. Enough had been accomplished to indicate that the potential of this great tool, educational television, had barely been realized. No longer an intriguing experiment, educational television had broken a trail that other nations had come to look upon with rapt interest.

Educational television represented a new challenge for the Peace Corps. Fortunately, such new challenges are continually arising as by-products of the fact that the Peace Corps exists. To put this another way, the fact that the Peace Corps exists generates astounding new impulses, new activities. I have mentioned how the Peace Corps is responding to what it was supposed to do, how it is responding to the three mandates laid down by Congress. I want to suggest some more new directions in which it is headed.

Most of these were undreamt of way back in that distant summer of 1961 when the first Peace Corps Volunteers went into training for Ghana, Colombia, Tanganyika (now part of Tanzania), and St. Lucia. A year from now, I am sure, a fresh set of remarkable enterprises will be in prospect. Every year since 1961, the Peace Corps has moved into new activities, such as educational television, which have more than surprised me—they have amazed me. I know why the Peace Corps was started; its purposes were spelled out by Congress. But every year since then, to paraphrase Volunteer David Ziegenhagen, I have been shown a dozen new reasons why it should have been established.

In 1964, for instance, Gene Bradley, a young General Electric executive in Schenectady, N. Y., wondered what to do with $750. The P.T.A. at Rosendale School, of which Bradley was president, had raised the money, but the school had no immediate need for it. A friend of Bradley's suggested to him, "Why don't you build a school abroad?" The friend explained that a school can be built in an overseas village for about a thousand dollars if the villagers will contribute the labor. Bradley took to the idea. Through the Peace Corps, he made contact with the small town of Casa Blanca, Colombia. The people of Casa Blanca thought it was a good idea, too, and agreed to raise the $250 still needed. They also agreed to supply the labor. The school of Casa Blanca is now built and in operation—but the story doesn't stop there. The Casa Blanca school children started a correspondence with the children at Rosendale, and this correspondence has continued. On the day that the school in Casa Blanca was finished, both schools held fairs where they featured articles made by each other.

Gene Bradley had seen from the first that the Peace Corps could play an essential role in what came to be known as the School-to-School program. I encouraged him to come to Peace Corps headquarters and develop the program from there. He obtained leave from General Electric, and within a few months, under his direction, thirty American schools had started the job of building an equal number of schools overseas. Another fifty had pledged to do so.

This was how the School-to-School program got started. It began when one American school reached a helping hand toward a village in distant Colombia. The existence of the Peace Corps meant that School-to-School could go into operation on a large scale with a minimum of fuss and red tape. Without the Peace Corps, an expansion of School-to-School would have been extremely difficult. Consider some

of the problems. After the children at an American school pledge themselves to raise a thousand dollars, what do they do next? How do they decide where an overseas school might be wanted or needed? Whom do they contact? How do they get materials to the construction site? Who can assure them that the townspeople will contribute their labor?

All these are questions that the Peace Corps can answer. Volunteers scattered around the globe know where school needs are greatest. In their roles as community development workers, Volunteers encourage self-help activities such as the contribution of labor. Often based in the faraway countryside, they are uniquely situated to act as middlemen between American schools and the people of remote villages.

School-to-School demonstrates that the Peace Corps spirit is not limited in America to those who join the Peace Corps. It offers a good example of how a first-rate idea, originating somewhere else in the American community, can be translated into reality with the assistance of the Peace Corps.

The Peace Corps has also been the receptacle of ideas that have originated overseas. An interesting example here can be found in the close working relationship that has developed between the Peace Corps and the Middle East Technical University in Ankara, Turkey.

Volunteers are never sent overseas without an assignment to organizations belonging to the country that invited them. Volunteers work for host-country "bosses," and not for other Americans. Peace Corps teachers, for example, work for the principals or headmasters of their schools. Peace Corps nurses work for the heads of the hospitals to which they are assigned. Agricultural extensionists—Volunteers who demonstrate farming skills—work for provincial or state supervisors and for the agriculture ministries of the nations to which they are assigned. Volunteers get a head start when their host organizations are dynamic and effective. This is the case with the Middle East Technical University.

Only a few years old, M.E.T.U. looks as if it will become the most important center for technical studies in the whole of the Near East. Its vast campus, covering barren hills on the southwestern edge of Turkey's capital city, is planted with more than a million yearling pine trees—including the John F. Kennedy Grove. New buildings and laboratories, many of them elaborately equipped, are rising on the campus under the command of the university's supercharged director, Kemal Kurdash. "Peace Corps teachers," Kurdash says, "are dynamic and effective, among the best teachers I have ever seen."

The books in M.E.T.U.'s technical libraries are written in English. Many of the university's lectures are in English. M.E.T.U.'s students must therefore have a mastery of English when they arrive. When it became apparent that his prospective students would not know enough English, Kurdash asked the Peace Corps for help. At his request, Volunteer Eugene Paslov (El Segundo, Calif.) prepared a prospectus for the Ford Foundation asking for money to establish an English preparatory school adjacent to M.E.T.U. The Ford Foundation responded with $150,000, which was used to build the prep school. Kurdash then asked Paslov to take over as one of the new school's two directors. Paslov did so, and went to work preparing courses and curricula designed to get his students into M.E.T.U. after one year of intensive English studies.

This school is now in operation, complete with classrooms and language laboratories. Helping Paslov handle his five hundred students are eighteen more Peace Corps teachers. In response to Kurdash's urgent requests, five more Peace Corps teachers, two with Ph.D. degrees, have joined the regular faculty of M.E.T.U. ,where they are now teaching scientific subjects.

Chances are excellent that the working relationship between M.E.T.U. and the Peace Corps will be even closer in the years ahead. The chances are also excellent that this university will become a true "light of Asia" and one of the great universities in the world. The Peace Corps will be able to say that it was there at the beginning, when it was needed. After testing its mettle with M.E.T.U., the Peace Corps is now ready to try similar relationships with other universities, both in Turkey and in other parts of the world.

These three examples—malaria eradication, the School-to-School program, the relationship with Middle East Technical University—indicate some of the new directions in which the Peace Corps is moving. All three are exciting to me because they put good ideas into action and because they open up new possibilities for the Peace Corps. All are moving along not as a result of spectacular breakthroughs but because dedicated people are carrying on the necessary day-to-day work.

Hard work is what has made the Peace Corps go. The largest overseas educational program in the history of the world is now being conducted by the Peace Corps in Africa. It functions because three thousand Volunteer teachers get up and go to their classes every weekday. It functions better than we had reason to hope because most of these three thousand men and women do much more than they are called on to do. Much of that extra work is still routine: teaching literacy classes, diligently coaching sports teams, organizing and cataloguing school libraries.

It seems strange that anyone would regard these unassuming, hard-working Peace Corps teachers as "the most dangerous opposition we have." But that is how the Chinese Communists think of them, according to a recent article in *Look* magazine. The author is Tung Chi-ping, a young Chinese diplomat who defected to the West after he had been assigned to the new African nation of Burundi. Getting ready to depart for Africa, Tung spoke with his superiors in Peking:

"I was encouraged to ask questions while preparing for my African trip and, naturally, I asked how influential Russia was in Africa. To my surprise, I was told that the Soviet Union had little influence there. Russia's efforts to infiltrate the new nations were sneered at by the African Affairs officials of the Foreign Ministry.

" 'A political vacuum exists in Africa,' they said. 'And we intend to fill it. Our enemy in Africa is not Russia but the United States. American agents under the name of the Peace Corps are the most dangerous opposition we have.' "

Communists have called Volunteers "spies" and "agents" since the Peace Corps was formed. Lately, their attacks have become less shrill as the charge has become less believable in Africa, Asia, and Latin America. Perhaps also they have become less strident as the Peace Corps idea has caught on. More than a dozen industrialized nations have already sent volunteers abroad as part of similar programs of their own, or have announced their intention to do so.

Our Volunteers are now welcoming these others as allies in the enduring struggle for a better life.

Meanwhile, American Peace Corps Volunteers will go on unself-consciously representing the finest qualities of free societies. That is probably why the Chinese find them so dangerous. Friendliness and understanding are the terrible weapons they wield.

In 1965, the Volunteers already so effective abroad, were just beginning to have their impact on the United States. I believe that the Volunteers, returning home in large numbers, will in time bring this nation its first large-scale understanding of the rest of the world, especially of the struggles and problems of huge populations which are on the path of development.

Just before Volunteer Ross Burkhardt (Central Valley, N. Y.) came home, he wrote, "Two years have passed; my life as a Peace Corps Volunteer has almost ended. On June 3, I fly from Tunis to Kennedy Airport and another world. Life will never again be the same. I leave part of myself here and I take part of Tunisia with me."

When Volunteer Jim Sheahan (Woonsocket, R. I.) prepared to return home from Sierra Leone, he received a tape from his colleagues at the Freetown radio station where he had worked as director of programs. He listened as a voice said, "Well, everybody, listen to me now. Our very good friend is going away. The few days that he spent with us are like five precious years. He is very quiet and every time you see him you look upon him as a son. He is always ready to give a pleasant answer to anybody who questions him. He is a real good soul—may he have long life and may he travel in peace."

A chorus then broke out in a song:

Mr. Sheahan, good-by; Mr. Sheahan, good-by.
We've come here now to say good-by to you . . .

Burkhardt, Sheahan, and thousand of others like them have resumed careers in the United States. In their two years overseas, they worked hard. They didn't transform the world. But they made a change in it. A hundred once-isolated villages in South America are now connected by roads to the outside world. A new chicken industry is thriving in the Punjab. Some Colombian villagers have tripled their incomes by exporting their handmade *ruanas* (poncho-like garments) as Volunteer Ron Atwater (Los Angeles) taught them to do.

The road to peace is built out of such small paving blocks as these, and a thousand more like them. This is why it is no broad and easy highway. It is narrow and winding; at one place, in the form of a real road, it crosses a bridge over a mountain torrent in Ecuador. Twenty farm families can now get their produce to market. The twenty families themselves built the bridge. A Peace Corps Volunteer worked alongside them.

The Peace Corps

Training

Every Peace Corps Volunteer is a graduate of a Peace Corps training program. Through the first four years of the Peace Corps no two training programs were exactly alike. Chances are good that they will never be standardized. This is because Peace Corps overseas programs are never quite the same; each new year makes its own unique demands, and training is tailored to each overseas program.

This has meant a lot of adjusting. In those first four years, the Peace Corps contracted for 470 different training programs at 86 colleges and universities

Top, a group of trainees in the Waipio Valley training center in Hawaii, fifty miles from Hilo. Behind the Volunteers, who will eventually go to Sabah and Sarawak, are dormitories built by earlier training groups in the style of houses of the Philippines and Thailand.

Waipio Volunteers training for Sarawak cut reeds to be used as roofing thatch for the Southeast Asian-type houses in which they will live.

Volunteers learn to plow a Hawaiian rice field with the only working water buffalo in the United States.

Trainees weed the project garden at the Waipio center.

in 32 states, the District of Columbia, Puerto Rico, and the Virgin Islands.

But for all their differences of detail, most training programs cover similar, basic ground. They all offer instruction directly related to the work to be done overseas. Community development workers, for example, are trained to use techniques they will use on the job. Prospective teachers get practice teaching and pedagogical technique courses as well as a survey of the syllabi and school systems of the nations they are headed for.

A trainee examines his freshly killed and plucked chicken at the Taos, New Mexico, camp.

Almost half of most training programs consists of language instruction. Sometimes a smattering of a second foreign language is offered after the trainees attain a standard level of proficiency with a first. Thus, Tunisia-bound Volunteers, trained in French, also get some instruction in Arabic.

The Peace Corps teaches a lot of languages. Some of them—French, Spanish, Portuguese—are familiar. Hardly as familiar to most Americans are languages such as Tagalog, Cebuano, Chabacano, Ilocano, Malay, Thai, Hindi, Panjabi, Kanarese, Gujerati, Bengali, Urdu, Nepali, Farsi, Turkish, Swahili, Amharic, Chinyanja, Ibo, Yoruba, Hausa, Djerma, Ewe, Twi, Somali, Wolof, Krio, Mendi, Temne, and Quechua. The training programs which offered these languages marked, in some instances, the first time they had ever been offered at an American university.

Other elements of training include a study of the history, culture, and customs of the country of destination, a survey of world political problems, a review of

American history, a look at special medical problems likely to be encountered—and a limited amount of physical education.

Many training programs have included

Training for a Latin-American health project, Volunteers register a baby's weight at a well-baby clinic at the New Mexico training center.

A hike in the wilderness east of Santa Fe, New Mexico, helps prepare Volunteers for Brazil.

four weeks of camp experience. Men and women headed for mountainous Nepal climbed the heights of Mt. Rainier in the State of Washington and attended the Outward Bound School in the Colorado Rockies. Many Volunteers headed for Latin America spent four weeks in either Camp Crozier or Camp Radley, both operated by the Peace Corps in tropical, mountainous country near Arecibo, Puerto Rico. Here, they got a look at a Spanish culture. They also participated as observers in Puerto Rico's own brilliantly conceived community development program, known as Operation Bootstrap.

Just as prospective Peace Corps teachers require practice teaching in training, so those going into community development work need an opportunity to do more than merely observe community development techniques. In 1963 the University of New Mexico agreed to conduct training in community development, with the academic parts of the program carried on at the campus in Albuquerque and the practical part among Spanish-speaking people in the northern part of the state. Those in training for other kinds of projects in Latin America continued to be sent to the camps in Puerto Rico.

Gradually over the winter of 1964–65 the camps became converted to another use. For some time the Peace Corps had been planning to carry out some training without the assistance of a college or university. The camps looked like the places to do this. Among other reasons for trying out the idea, the agency wanted to see if training could be improved with a permanent staff continually concerned with increasing efficiency. This staff was gradually brought together. And after February 1, 1965, no one was sent to the camps except for the full training period, usually twelve weeks.

In June, 1963, another camp was opened in Hawaii for Volunteers headed for the Far East. In the lush but almost deserted Waipio Valley on the island of Hawaii,

Top, preparing for community development work in Colombia, trainees from the Taos, New Mexico, center help a farmer build another room on his house out of adobe bricks. The trainees spend several days at a time working in the small Spanish-speaking villages around Taos.

Roping down a sheer cliff is a regular training routine at the New Mexico center.

an Asian village was constructed in replica, complete with terraced rice fields and the only working water buffalo in the United States. The camp was administered by the University of Hawaii, whose staff also handled the academic training, usually at the Hilo campus, for the men and women before they completed their training with four weeks at Waipio.

Somehow word was circulated that training for the Peace Corps was tougher than training for the Marines. The story went that those in training were forced to drop by rope over the awesome face of Puerto Rico's huge Dos Bocas dam, that they had to learn to swim with their hands and feet tied, that they were sent through mountains and jungle on four-day survival treks. The fact is that these stories were true. And yet Peace Corps camp training, based on the philosophy of Outward Bound, is nothing at all like Marine Corps training.

In the first place, many Volunteers are older, some in their sixties and seventies, and they are not subjected to physical training demands which they cannot readily fulfill. Staying afloat in water with hands and feet tied is a trick that prospective Volunteers are taught to do while receiving instruction in "drown-proofing." These survival swimming techniques were developed by Fred Lanoue, swimming coach at the University of Alabama and the first swimming instructor at the Puerto Rico camps. Volunteers are not asked to "pass" drown-proofing as if it were a test. They are asked to do the best they can with it, just as they are with all other elements of the camp experience. If they succeed and manage to swim with their hands and feet tied, they gain a measure of confidence, which is the essence of Outward Bound. They have placed themselves in a totally strange situation and found that they could handle it. This is part of their preparation for facing strange situations overseas. It is a proper goal of Peace Corps training, which is not designed to produce muscle men.

But not all training includes camp experience. Although Camp Crozier was inaugurated by the first group headed for

Trainees do the Filipino "bird dance," performed between two long poles kept in continual motion.

Tanganyika, few Volunteers now in Africa were sent to camp. Most of them, as well as most Volunteers in the Near East and South Asia, took all twelve weeks of their training on the campus of a stateside university or at such institutions as the Experiment in International Living at Putney, Vermont. But even these Volunteers received some kind of field experience, if only in the neighborhood of the training campus.

And camp or no, the pressure was on them just as it is on all men and women who undergo Peace Corps training. They will not be Peace Corps Volunteers until they have finished training, and about 20 per cent of those who begin fail to finish. Of those who don't make it, many decide on their own that the Peace Corps is not for them. Others are sent home by the field selection boards which are charged with eliminating those who, in their

opinion, won't turn into good Volunteers.

In the academic phase of training, prospective Volunteers are typically in class for sixty hours every week. In twelve weeks, they usually get three hundred hours of language, and sometimes more, equivalent to at least two years of college work. Few of them have studied this intensely before. On top of this—the demand for a supreme effort on their part—they have the knowledge that they will soon be leaving everything that is familiar to them, home, family, and friends—if they make it—and setting off for a strange and distant place. Training is tough and it is often tense. Yet by 1964, more than five thousand men and women were getting through it every year and emerging from the process as full-fledged Peace Corps Volunteers.

Top, Mohammad Mohiyud-Din of the East Pakistan Education Service conducts a lesson in Bengali for trainees at the Experiment in International Living in Putney, Vermont.

At the Putney, Vermont, training center, a Volunteer bound for Africa receives language instruction from a Guinean teacher.

Latin America

The preliminaries were over: training, the flight to Bogotá, and a week of orientation in the capital city. Two community development Volunteers found themselves at last on their own in the town of Sandoná in southwestern Colombia. "We looked around at the two-foot-thick walls of our adobe house," said Stephen Murray of Park Ridge, Illinois. "At the door, the only opening in the walls, villagers were clustered, staring at the strangers. *'¿Como amaneció? ¿Como le va yendo? ¿Se amaña?'* My nerves froze as I realized I couldn't understand them."

Murray was one of sixty-two Volunteers, all men, who were sent to Colombia in October, 1961, to inaugurate the Peace Corps' first community development program. He had had only sixty hours of Spanish language training (his successors now receive more than five times this much). But Murray and his partner, Jim Gregory (Longmont, Colo.), had the assistance of Miguel, their Colombian co-worker, "who had the patience to teach us the colloquial Spanish of Sandoná."

As a member of a pioneer group, Murray had few guidelines to tell him how to carry out community development. It had been described to him as social work but not casework; entire communities were to be the objects of its efforts. Community development is the chief area of Peace Corps work in Latin America. Volunteers are sent to live in rural villages and urban slums, where they encourage the inhabitants to organize and improve their lives through their own efforts. It is new and it is exciting. When properly carried out, community development takes hold where other forms of aid are ignored or scorned. This is because it is not just aid; it is self-help, and the recipients are involved in bringing it about with their own thought and their own sweat.

When Murray and Gregory arrived in Colombia, no one knew if Volunteers could do community development. Two weeks after they arrived, as Murray reported, they found that "we were still in a goldfish bowl. You would think that the novelty of two *norteamericanos* would wear off. But, no, we had twenty-two visitors this evening, and the Mayor has invited us out for a drink."

Not only the inhabitants of Sandoná had their eyes on these young men; in a sense, all of Latin America was watching them. If the Volunteers proved their ability to be of use, Latin America would want lots of them.

Members of this first Colombia group made many mistakes while, in a sense, they wrote in action the basic Peace Corps textbook on community development. The Colombians were tolerant of errors. Within a short time, Colombia had become enthusiastic. Making a speech in 1963, Colombia's President, Dr. Guillermo León Valencia, paused to make "special honorable mention of that gallant legion of American young men, who in furthering the Alliance for Progress under the noble title of 'The Peace Corps,' have launched out ... to every corner of [Latin] America to study, understand and help her. ... They make direct contact with our most humble people in our towns and villages; they hear their complaints, understand their anguish and stimulate their hopes. There is no other action more effective to the service of continental integration than this Peace Corps which allows a young man from Chicago to know the thoughts of a man from Sabanalarga or Firavitoba. ..."

As President Valencia noted, community development Volunteers had gone to all parts of Latin America by the time he made those remarks. And not just young men, but young women had gone, too, and older Volunteers. They had been assigned to villages scattered through six thousand miles of country, from Guatemala to southern Chile, from the seacoast bulge of Ecuador to the slum *favelas* of Rio de Janeiro. They went to work where they were assigned to live, in almost a thousand villages and in the waterless shantytowns ringing almost all of Latin America's big cities—Santiago, Lima, Arequipa, Rio de Janeiro, Guayaquil, Quito, Bogotá, Caracas. They made new friends in both city and village, and they could be found in tropical America's endless summer, working, talking, laughing.

For all its excitement and drama, community development when seen from the lonely perspective of the remote Volunteer in his isolated village is more often an exercise in plain hard work, in frustration, sometimes in heartbreak. The successes tend to be publicized, while the ordinary community development worker may be encountering a seemingly endless series of setbacks. He reads of the triumphs of others sometimes with wry amusement, sometimes with a kind of mounting guilt. And yet his effect on his own village or city slum is usually visible to more detached observers. The cumulative impact of thousands of community development Volunteers is beginning to generate a revolution of self-help among millions of people.

In some ways, community development is a Peace Corps activity *par excellence*. Volunteers assigned to other activities almost inevitably find themselves involved in some form of community development in the off-hours projects which they set for themselves. For although most of the Volunteers in Latin America are placed in some kind of community development, quite a number are assigned to other types of programs. To cite figures, at the beginning of 1965 in Latin America (including English-speaking St. Lucia, Jamaica, and British Honduras), thirty-five hundred Volunteers were at work. Of these, about two thousand were primarily assigned to community development programs in sixteen countries: Guatemala, British Honduras, Honduras, El Salvador, Costa Rica, Panama, the Dominican Republic, Jamaica, St. Lucia, Brazil, Venezuela, Colombia, Ecuador, Peru, Bolivia, and Chile. The other fifteen hundred were involved in more than thirty fields of endeavor.

The second largest Volunteer activity in Latin America is agriculture, carried out usually by demonstrations in the field, as in Uruguay, and often blending into rural community development to the point where the two can't be distinguished. Still other Volunteers are teaching in universities in Chile, Peru, Ecuador, Colombia, Venezuela, Brazil, and Central America. Teaching programs have also been mounted in physical education, in vocational education, and—in a very limited way—in secondary schools. Volunteer foresters are at work in Peru. Volunteer construction teams are building schools in Ecuador. Volunteer accountants are forming cooperatives for production, sales, and credit on South America's west coast and in Panama. Volunteer health teams are working in sanitation, nutrition, and medical programs in Chile, Peru, Bolivia, Colombia, and Brazil.

Latin America has also provided the setting for some trail-blazing programs which have expanded the range of Peace Corps activities into surprising areas. In Colombia, a teacher shortage was circumvented by South America's first nation-spanning educational television system, installed and put into operation with the help of Volunteers. In Ecuador and in Brazil's São Paulo State, Volunteers are hastening rural electrification. In Ecuador, Peru, and Colombia, Volunteers skilled in arts and crafts are assisting cottage industries, enrolling local craftsmen into cooperatives, and finding markets for their products. In Peru, community development workers are doing something quite special: working in the country's National Peruvian Plan for Integration of Andean Indians.

But community development is the inescapable subject in Latin America, involving Volunteers in many special projects. Peace Corps men and women are at work in the area called the Alto Beni of Bolivia, helping in a government program to resettle Indians from the high Altiplano into the lush lowlands of the upper Amazon. In Chile, so far south that Volunteers are sometimes snowbound in July blizzards, they have worked out a poultry program to supplement all-potato diets with eggs.

The ordinary things they are expected to do are also done despite setbacks and frustration. Stephen Murray and his group of sixty-two, the pioneers, working out their techniques as they went along, finding out the hard way what they could and could not do, managed to get quite a bit accomplished. In the twenty-one months they were in Colombia, they helped build forty-four rural schools and began an additional fifty-five. They helped to construct two hundred miles of rural roads, often involving bridges. They built twenty-seven aqueducts and started work on twenty-nine more. They saw the completion of four health centers and the start of thirteen others. They instituted latrine programs in thirty-three areas and got more than a thousand latrines installed. They helped establish twenty-six cooperatives, built farm ponds and stocked them with fish, helped build sports fields and recreation areas, and, in their extra time, coached sports teams and started adult literacy programs. They would have accomplished much more if results were all that they were seeking. But expediency was less important than another goal: the Volunteer had been summoned to work through the slower paths of self-help.

Tom Carter (Portland, Ore.) explained this challenge and dilemma while describing his life as a community development Volunteer in one of the *barriadas*, or slums, surrounding the coastal city of Chimbote in Peru:

"In [one] *barriada* in my town, there are two schools. One is a several-thousand-dollar complex with classrooms, meeting halls, and a medical clinic. It was built by Peace Corps Volunteers: architects labored with social workers pouring cement, laying concrete blocks, putting in lights and plumbing. It is now completed and in partial use. Peruvians call it 'the gringo school.'

"Next door to this complex stands a two-room school, built out of grass mats, without windows or lights, and a dirt floor. It was built because the *barriada* grew and because classroom space was needed. The teacher, a Peace Corps Volunteer, talked the parents of the students into building those two rooms. I consider the grass school a success, and ten times more valuable to the community than the big complex it sits next to. It will remain a symbol to the *barriada* people of what *they* can do—working together. . . .

"A really good Peace Corps program receives little credit. Keep that in mind when you read Peace Corps success stories. . . . I have a lot of failures, few tangible successes, and a great deal of frustration. (I was a dreamer once, too, and my fall was hard.) Now, all things considered, I think I'm doing something worthwhile. I don't think I'll sign up for another stretch, but you couldn't drag me away from this one."

Bolivia

Wherever the New World promised gold, thither the Spanish went. In 1538, after the conquest of Peru, Hernando Pizarro and his men pressed south into the high Andean region we know today as Bolivia. There, in what was the southern sector of the fallen Inca Empire, he found gold. With the colonization that followed, and with the development of farms, textile mills, and mines, another rivulet joined the stream of wealth flowing into the Spanish treasury. To labor in the colonists' mines and fields became the obligation of the defeated Indians.

Although during the sixteenth and seventeenth centuries Bolivia grew into a land of fabled wealth and, until the eighteenth century, Potosí, the principal mining center, was the largest city in the New World, the easy riches yielded by those mines of early days have long since disappeared. As the gold veins dwindled the Spanish colonists turned more and more to agriculture and a semifeudal hacienda society evolved. This manorial system of

Spanish landholders and Indian serfs (*campesinos*) proved remarkably stable. In spite of violent Indian uprisings in the eighteenth century, an extended war for independence from Spain (independence was gained in 1825), disastrous border wars (Bolivia lost her access to the sea to Chile in the War of the Pacific, 1879–1884), and a stormy political life (179 revolutions), the system persisted until 1952, when by government decree the large estates were broken up and the land redistributed among the peasants. Today agriculture is the dominant economic activity with over 70 per cent of Bolivia's population engaged in farming. The country's great mineral wealth is an insult to her people: over the years deposits of tin, silver, zinc, copper, lead, antimony, bismuth, wolfram, and iron—some of great magnitude—have been discovered and exploited. But the mines, owned by the government and controlled by powerful, self-interested unions, are unable to operate at a profit. This potentially important industry contributes little to alleviating poverty in the majority of the people—the small farmers.

An Aymara Indian village with its houses of thatch and stone on Bolivia's Altiplano. The bleak landscape is typical of the broad plateau, which at altitudes above 11,000 feet lies between two gigantic mountain chains of the Andes.

The geographical key to Bolivia is the Altiplano, a broad, windswept plateau over five hundred miles long, cradled between two great mountain chains; for the western third of the land perches high in the Andes—the Tibet of South America—and holds the bulk of her population (over 3,500,000). Most Bolivians live two miles above sea level, some dwelling at altitudes above sixteen thousand feet. To the east the land descends into a vast drainage basin of tributaries to the Amazon, a region of rain forests and sparse settlement. The Altiplano is inhabited by the Aymaras, the mountains by Quechuas, both important tribes in the ancient Inca Empire. These are the small farmers. The people of Spanish descent, who make up only 13 per cent of the population, reside in the cities and are engaged in business, trade, and industry.

Into this high-altitude and essentially agrarian milieu the Peace Corps Volunteer comes, and he encounters there the conditions that mark most economically underdeveloped nations: illiteracy, hunger, disease, inadequate medical services, lack of sanitation facilities, primitive housing, a shortage of skilled manpower, poor transportation and communications, ancient farming techniques, and—the greatest obstacle of all—a resistance, bound up by customs and traditions, to modern improvements.

Habits impede change, especially when they are embedded in physical hardship; routine can be an insulating film, and on the Bolivian Altiplano the film is tainted with narcotics. Chewing the coca leaf, from which cocaine derives, is common among the Indians. Its soporific effects dull hunger and deaden the nerves to pain. It can make one impervious to the cold wind and the gloom of a mean existence. It puts on the face of the user a blank, uncomprehending stare. The drug has a long history of use in the Andes (*coca* is a Quechua word), and it is an inextricable component of Aymara and Quechua cul-

Farmers of the Altiplano follow an old superstition at planting time. The white flags are thought to ward off evil spirits. The farmers' chief crops are wheat, potatoes, barley, and corn.

At an altitude of 16,000 feet Aymara Indians plant potatoes in a cloud-wreathed mountain pass near La Paz, Bolivia's capital. Women work the fields side by side with the men.

An Aymara Indian huddles in the cold of an Altiplano afternoon outside his hut.

Inside the same hut, the desperately ill son of the man in the picture above is treated by Peace Corps nurses Nancy Crawford and Mary Cross.

ture. It is part of the web of circumstance within which the Peace Corps must operate in Bolivia.

Working under the auspices of the Bolivian government, Peace Corps Volunteers are mounting their attack against these conditions on four fronts: health, agriculture, colonization, and university projects.

To the cold, monotonous Altiplano the Peace Corps has sent nurses, teachers, community development workers, and agriculture extension agents to live and work among the *campesinos*. For many of these people, so far removed from modern civilization with its conveniences and horrors, the presence of Peace Corps Volunteers has meant the first medical attention they have ever received.

Volunteer nurses Nancy Crawford (Rumford, R.I.) and Mary Cross (Ridgefield, Wash.) started their own clinic in the small town of Peñas. The two Volunteers lived in a tiny room off the village plaza. Next door, in a slightly larger room, they set up the clinic. There were no doctors in the town, which has a population of about

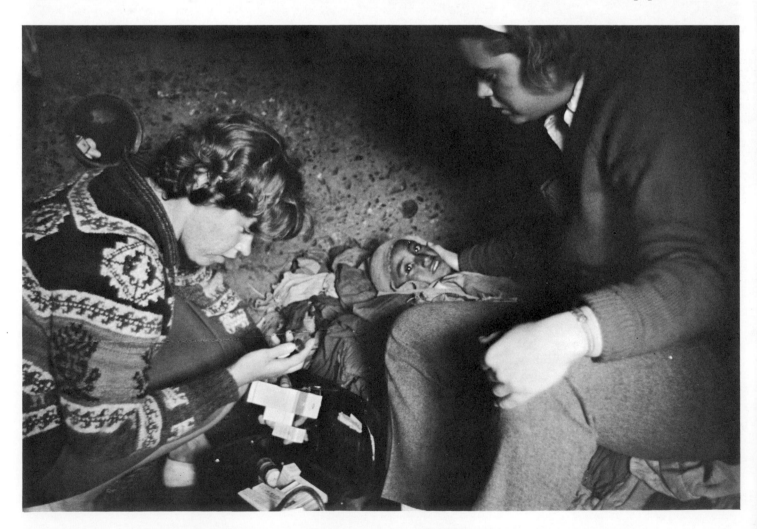

An elderly Aymara woman wearing her black bowler. The bowlers are worn almost universally by Indian women, a convention of uncertain origin. Quechua women wear white bowlers.

Above right, a young Aymara woman of the Cochabamba valley.

Right, campesinos plod along under heavy burdens in La Paz.

A business street in La Paz. The city is situated at an altitude of 11,900 feet.

Volunteer Prudence Ingerman (Carversville, Pa.) conducts an outdoor arithmetic class for first-graders in La Paz.

School construction workers pause for lunch with Volunteer James Allen (Bunkerhill, Ill.) in a poorer district of La Paz. The Bolivian men are unemployed factory workers who agreed to help build the school for their daily meals.

6,000. The people of Peñas and those in the surrounding area became totally dependent upon the two nurses and their meager medical supplies. Several days a week Nancy and Mary set out in their jeep to nearby villages where they held clinics. At times an entire village would line up for treatment.

In the past Peñas' water had had to be hauled from a distant well. While the Volunteers were there, a source of good water was discovered close by. The two nurses encouraged the villagers to make the small payment necessary to have water piped into their homes and, to set an example, had water piped into the clinic and their own quarters. They even dug their own trench for the water pipe.

Throughout Bolivia—in the Altiplano, in the mountains and valleys, and in the eastern lowlands, where resettlement projects are under way—Peace Corps Volunteers have been engaged in such seemingly rudimentary (but revolutionary to the Bolivians) projects as constructing latrines, giving health instruction to children in primary schools, conducting nursing aid courses, drilling wells, developing upright cooking stoves, and organizing Girl Scout troops, boys' clubs, civic action committees, and young adult groups. And in their spare time, Volunteers introduce recreational programs and facilities to people accustomed to accepting poverty apathetically.

Bolivia has nothing to compare with the urban slums of Lima in Peru or Rio in Brazil. Her principal cities, La Paz, the capital, and Cochabamba, have not drawn the rural people to settle in shacks on their outskirts. But La Paz, like major cities around the world, has her poor and destitute. To these people the Peace Corps has brought teachers. To the farmers who hold land near the cities the Volunteers have introduced new possibilities for growing marketable crops and new ways of bringing their produce to the cities. Few farmers grow enough on their land to feed their own families; those who do produce a small surplus laboriously haul it on their backs for miles to market.

The government's agrarian reform program, begun in 1952, achieved the desired result of putting land in the hands of the peasants. But it failed in its more important goal: to increase food production. In fact, production has declined. The peasant, often illiterate, unmotivated, unacquainted with the abstractions of marketing and finance, does not see beyond the boundaries of his little plot of land and the immediate needs of his family. The result is that this overwhelmingly agricultural country has to import 50 per cent of her food.

Comprising about two thirds of the land surface, the eastern lowlands in Bolivia would seem to offer solutions to many problems. River transportation for the movement of produce, unused arable land, ample rainfall, and room for expansion are all available there. To take advantage of this natural bounty of land the Bolivian government has encouraged

Top, a resettlement village in the Alto Beni, a sector in Bolivia's eastern lowlands. Indians are encouraged by the government to move into the fertile and potentially productive lowlands from the barren Altiplano and the mountains.

Volunteer Robert Kelly (Carlsbad, Calif.) pitches in to mix cement with two Alto Beni settlers. The cement was poured to make a floor for a chicken house. Rhode Island Red chicks were shipped in from the United States to establish chicken propagation farms in the new colony.

goal of five years of subsistence agriculture and consolidation of the community, after which permanent crops such as cocoa, coffee, and citrus fruit would be introduced. The Peace Corps' task was to aid the Bolivian technical staff in agriculture, construction, architecture, and social work.

Volunteers like Denis Regan (New York City) and Mickey Melragon (Columbus, Ohio) perceived the need for roads in the Alto Beni region and, borrowing a tractor from the road service, built seven miles of access roads into the farms. Other Volunteers started a chicken and pig propagation and distribution project. Two engineers and a draftsman supervised construction of the main camp.

Such were the first jobs undertaken by the Volunteers in the Alto Beni project. Before long they recognized their mistake, a mistake repeated many times by the Peace Corps in these years of experimentation: the Volunteers had moved into the community, decided what it needed most, and pursued action *by their own labor* to correct the needs. Instead, the Volunteers should have pointed out the community

Work nears completion on a 4,000-gallon water tower at a work camp deep in the rain forests of the upper Amazon drainage basin. Roy Griffith (New York City), standing center, designed the tower.

A Bolivian farmer watches as Volunteers Mickey Melragon, right, and Denis Regan, center, show him how to plant fruit trees in a resettlement farm.

small farmers of the Altiplano to pull up roots and resettle in the east. The Peace Corps has been invited to send Volunteers to the resettlement villages to help clear land, set up community organizations, and convert the settlers to the idea of growing crops that have no immediate relationship to their hunger but that may be sent to market for money. To convince these settlers that a cocoa plant can support them better than a potato plant is to convince them of the efficacy of a new magic.

Following Indians who have already settled there, Peace Corps Volunteers live

and work in pioneer communities like a project in the Alto Beni, a region around the Beni River, approximately a hundred miles northeast of La Paz. Penetration roads have crept over the eastern cordillera and have reached valleys in the fertile foothills. They will soon reach the open plains. When Volunteers first arrived at the Alto Beni project they found about five hundred families settled in the area, which had been opened up only eighteen months before. The Bolivian Development Corporation, the government agency directing the project, had planned on a needs to the settlers, helped them to organize a plan of action, developed and encouraged leaders, educated, trained, and persuaded, and then worked alongside the settlers to achieve the goals. Only through a program of education and organization, and by a development of leaders, can a community—urban or rural—become self-sustaining and independent of outside help.

Volunteers are, of course, sensitive to errors. A Volunteer report from the Alto Beni reads in part: "The Alto Beni project has had only mixed success for a number of reasons. We were not conscious of the delicate balance between doing as much as possible in any way possible and fulfilling the Volunteer's true role as an organizer of human rather than material resources. The results of our work in the Alto Beni have largely been material; we have only had partial success in the changing of attitudes and ideas. Economically, the region has advanced considerably, but the communities are still not self-reliant."

While the pioneer communities rise in the eastern foothills and lowlands and migrants trickle along the new roads, Bolivia's 3,500,000 people remain essentially stationary—on the Altiplano, in the highlands, and in mountain valleys. Advances in health, agriculture, and community development are needed there more than ever; the need will continue for a long time to come.

Peace Corps nurses and agricultural workers have been active in the farming communities in valleys around Cochabamba, Bolivia's second largest city. In the Cochabamba area alone, thousands of people have been vaccinated against various diseases. With the cooperation of Heifer Project, Inc., a nondenominational Christian organization set up to distribute high-quality livestock around the world, the Volunteers attempt to improve herds

Top, in the town of Tiquipaya in the Cochabamba valley, nurses Nancy Turner (Gary, N. C.), left, and Lois Duffin (Alameda, Calif.), right, stop to admire a baby slung on the back of a Quechua Indian mother.

Volunteer Ben Brackin (What Cheer, Iowa), left, and a Bolivian co-worker make preparations for reading a tuberculin test they had given to a cow on a Cochabamba valley farm. Farmers were warned not to use the milk of infected cows in a campaign to eradicate tuberculosis in the valley's dairy herds.

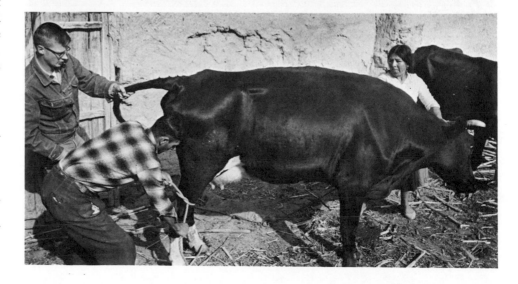

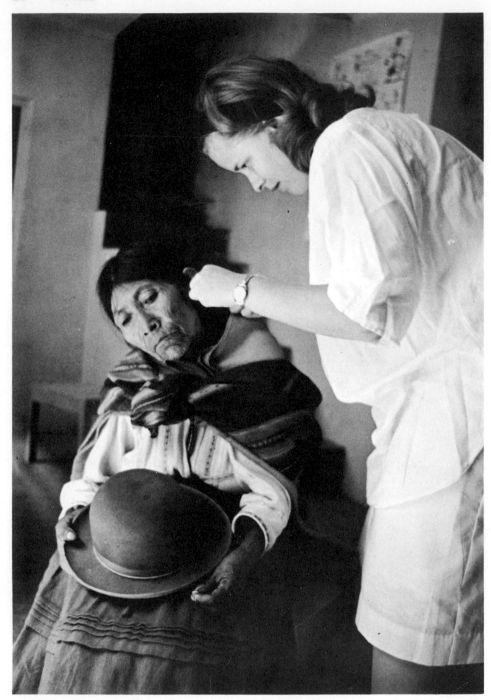

families. Intestinal parasites and tuberculosis were the diseases the nurses encountered most frequently in their rounds. They did their best to persuade mothers that children should drink boiled water and wear shoes, and sleep in separate beds if they were tubercular.

Keeping in sight the high goals they brought with them, the nurses were quite capable of making realistic assessments of their work. Said Priscilla Bauguess, "The results of our work, if there are any, will come years from now. You can't really cure the sick here because you can't control their environment. Who can blame them for not taking everything we say seriously? If I were a *campesino*, I would think you were crazy if you told me there were dangerous bugs in a clear-looking glass of water. . . . All we can really do is to try and help them and let them know somebody really cares about them."

Sustained progress can only come with conversion. No government agency nor any number of Peace Corps Volunteers can revolutionize Bolivian society. But the good word can be broadcast.

In her clinic in the town of Coroico, Priscilla Bauguess treats an Indian woman for an ear infection.

A young Indian boy receives consolation from Priscilla Bauguess after she had treated him for a fever. Priscilla was on her way to make a house call when the boy's mother, squatting in the doorway, stopped her and asked for help.

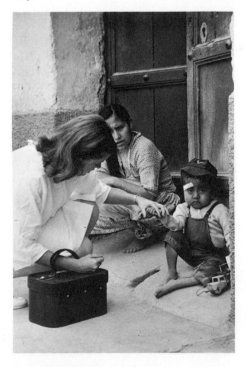

by educating farmers in the care and feeding of farm animals.

A few head of sheep and cattle of good stock have been brought in to strengthen herds, but improvements will be mainly accomplished by promoting animal husbandry techniques among herdsmen and dairymen. They must be persuaded to accept these techniques and, if the Volunteers' work is not in vain, to use them after the Peace Corps is gone.

Progress may be slow, but in the meantime Volunteers can bring some measure of immediate help to an ailing people, especially with medical care. Priscilla

Bauguess (Chicago), a Peace Corps Volunteer nurse, helped to check a yellow fever epidemic in eastern Bolivia by inoculating nearly four thousand people within two weeks. The redheaded nurse rode a mule from village to village over slippery, muddy roads. Later, she and Blanch Lonski (Kensal, N. D.) were assigned to the mountain town of Coroico (population 7,500), where they set up a clinic in the rear of a church.

No one in Coroico or in the surrounding countryside, other than the two young Americans, was qualified to give medical treatment to the *campesinos* and their

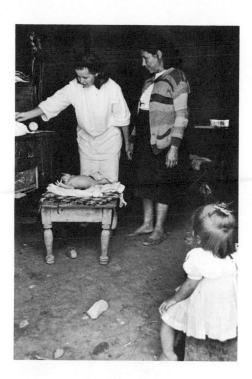

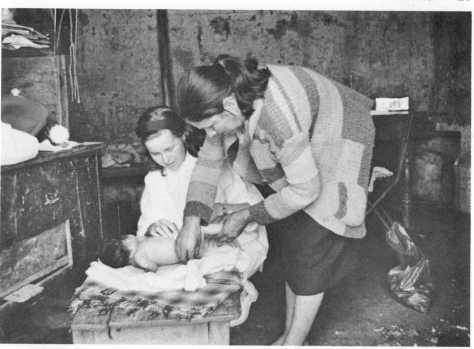

Above, instruction in bathing a newborn baby . . . and practice for the mother.

During a respite from work, Priscilla Bauguess stops to converse with two Aymara women in Spanish. Although the Aymara language con- *tinues to be spoken, the Aymaras have borrowed many words and constructions from Spanish.*

Peru

Lima, Peru, stands among the queens of South American cities. She is cultured, urbane, and proud of her Iberian heritage. She rivals her Spanish ancestors in grandeur and surpasses them in vigor and progress. Old World beauty, romance, and guitar music fuse with broad avenues and skyscrapers in a luminous synthesis. But the gay queen is vexed by a disconcerting blemish: she is encircled by horrendous slums.

Probably the first word a Peru-bound Volunteer puts into his Spanish vocabulary is *barriada*. It means "shantytown" or "squatter settlement." Indians by the

Top, Peruvian misery. This is reputed to be the worst slum in South America—shacks of tar paper and tin on the outskirts of Lima.

Comas, one of the many barriadas *ringing Lima. The people have simply invaded the land, squatted on it, and thrown up ramshackle dwellings.*

thousands come down from the mountains to squat on government-owned land and erect flimsy houses of mud, cane, and tin. They live in unimaginable squalor, hoping some day, somehow, to be assimilated by the prosperity of the city. From their hovels—built sometimes upon a mountain of garbage—they can see the glittering tiara of modern Lima. Swarming *barriadas* surround every major Peruvian city—Lima, Arequipa, Trujillo, Callao—and the smaller cities as well—Cajamarca, Piura, Chimbote, Huancayo, and Ayacucho.

The prospect of an American setting up house in a filthy *barriada*—no sanitary facilities, no sewers, no running water—will cancel much of the romance associated with Peace Corps work. Yet hundreds of Americans have done just that: they have moved into Peru's squatter communities, living with Indian families, occupying vacant quarters, or building rooms for themselves. (Some of the early Volunteers erected luxurious, by *barriada* standards,

Martha Iwaski stands in the doorway of a barriada school in the coastal city of Chimbote. The children are holding their one hot meal of the day—breakfast.

Volunteer nurse Robin Adams (Escondido, Calif.) attends to a cut hand in her small clinic in Chimbote. Clinic equipment and drugs came from Pensacola, Fla., through the People-to-People program.

Along the Pacific, children from a Chimbote school run with their teacher Lois Fenzl (Schenectady, N. Y.).

Below right, Greg Labuza (Perth Amboy, N. J.) gives a reading lesson to three Chimbote children. At the Volunteer's suggestion, neighborhood fathers built the thatched structure in which clases were held.

A class of Chimbote boys learns the fundamentals of batting from Volunteer Joe Grant (Bronx, N. Y.).

domiciles, which set them apart from the squatters. To avoid ill feelings, the Volunteers eventually vacated these quarters and turned them over to community organizations.) They make their simple residences as clean and as comfortable as possible and practice good health and hygiene habits. All Volunteers, whether they are nurses, teachers, tradesmen, architects, draftsmen, engineers, or community development workers, help the

squatters in this indirect way—they set an example.

Like many others throughout the country, the squatter settlements in Chimbote, a northern coastal city, have received attention from the Peruvian government and the Peace Corps. Martha Iwaski (Santa Fe, N. M.) was one of several Volunteers there representing the government's National School Feeding Plan (Plan Nacional de Alimentación Escolar).

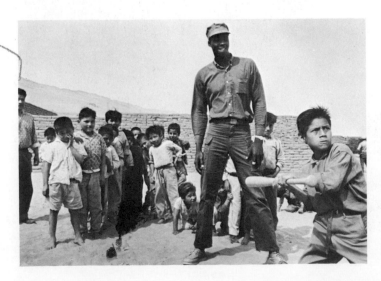

Pupils discuss a lesson with their teacher, Catherine Cramer (Los Angeles), in Peravillo, a squatter community fifty miles north of Lima. Catherine's school had a floor of sand, walls of straw matting, and no roof. Classes in the open-sky schoolhouse were not inhibited by the elements, for Peravillo is situated in a desert region where rain almost never falls.

Above right, Volunteer Cramer and her companion teacher, Gail Engles (New York City), oversee their pupils at play.

Gail Engles guides one of her young students through a lesson in her roofless classroom.

The objective of the Plan is to see that every Peruvian school child gets at least one hot meal a day. Martha and another Volunteer managed a hot breakfast program for four thousand pupils in Chimbote. The Volunteers spent their mornings visiting schools to see that the food was properly served. Some of the food (powdered milk, corn meal, shortening) is donated by the United States Food for Peace program, and cooking utensils, the administrative framework, and Peruvian food products (sugar, cocoa, wheat) are supplied by the Peruvian government.

The National School Feeding Plan is an integral part of a scheme to promote education. It improves the nutrition of thousands of children and it invites the cooperation of parents; the hope is that school enrollment will increase. Government officials fully realize that education is the only final answer to the squatter situation.

A Quechua Indian campesino pauses with his load. He is standing in Peru's Urubamba valley, near Cuzco, the ancient capital of the Inca Empire. In the background can be seen a mission church and the Andes.

Barriada children will waste away in melancholy, just as their parents have done, unless they learn to read and write and acquire a negotiable skill. Hot meals will help, but to make Peru's compulsory education laws more than expressions of good intentions schools will have to be built and teachers trained. At the government's request, the Peace Corps has dispatched construction workers, plasterers, plumbers, electricians, and teachers to the *barriadas.*

Building a school, the Peace Corps found out early in Peru, can be done in two ways: the easy way and the hard way. Most Volunteers agree that in the *barriadas* the hard way is better. In the easy way, Peace Corps Volunteers build the school. In the hard way, the *barriada* people build it.

The hard way is better. Why? Because the slum dwellers must make themselves independent. They have to be made to realize that with their own efforts, their

A young Quechua mother, with a child slung on her back, and her small flock of llamas. The llamas are beasts of burden but obstinately refuse to carry more than one hundred pounds. The woman's hands busily prepare wool for spinning.

own skills, their own resources, they can direct their fate.

Volunteer Tom Carter (Portland, Ore.) taught school in a Chimbote slum. He taught carpentry at night. His school had no roof. "It would be a ten-dollar project and about one day's labor for two or three Peace Corpsmen to build that roof," he said during his tour in Chimbote. "Yet we don't do it. If we gave my school a roof, it would always be that, a gift, the gringo's roof. When it needed fixing, no one would fix it. If it takes me a year to talk my neighbors into putting on that roof, it will be worth it. . . . Because it will then be *their* roof on *their* school. It will be a small start, but in the right direction."

The *barriadas* are the visible social problem in Peru. Prosperous city dwellers encounter the uncomfortable facts daily. But the *barriadas* are only a symptom. For the cause one must ascend the Andes, which dominate two thirds of the Peruvian land area. Millions of Indians, descendants of the Incas, are scattered among these mighty mountains. They lead a harsh agri-

cultural existence relieved only by the annual fiesta. They may own a little land, on which they grow potatoes and grain, or a few head of livestock, llamas or sheep, but the crop yield is low and families are undernourished. Compared to their Inca ancestors, who understood and applied the principles of irrigation, fertilization, and terracing, their agricultural techniques are backward. They speak Quechua or Aymara, ancient tongues of the Incas, a major obstacle between them and their Spanish-speaking government. They are illiterate and do not know how to protect themselves against disease. Life expectancy is only thirty-two years. As rental payment on land they work for themselves, many Indians are obliged to labor three or four days a week for owners of large estates. Such is the world the *barriada* people are running away from.

Distributed over wide areas in the titanic Andes, penetrating the remotest

A fiesta scene in the Andean mountain town of Urubamba. Watching the masked dancers and paraders is Anna Acitelli (Painesville, Ohio), who worked in Urubamba as the associate director of a teacher's college.

A saucy young Quechua girl, wearing her distinctive wide-brimmed hat. She lives in the Peruvian market town of Pisac, near Cuzco.

trails and reaching hamlets that until recently might have been on another planet for all their contact with the outside world, Peace Corps Volunteers work and hope. They have accepted part of an immense assignment: to help five million Indians lift themselves out of semiconscious desperation. Farmers, nurses, literacy instructors, auto mechanics, welders, carpenters, social workers, teachers, anthropologists, and others strike out from home villages or towns to offer a lesson, an idea, a hot meal, a helping hand.

With majestic scenery and *plein air*, an assignment in the highlands would seem preferable to the *barriadas*, but Volunteers in the Andes are often withered by frustration. Working as agents of Peru's National Peruvian Plan for Integration of Andean Indians, they have to cope with bureaucratic entanglements and poor communications. Requests for supplies or information from Lima tend to be delayed or get lost. As one prominent Peruvian explained, "You will learn that *underdevelopment* means not just that the Indian is poor; the term applies to every level of our society. That's one of the basic reasons you are here."

For most Volunteers in the Andes, work has proceeded at a turtle's pace, and it will not accelerate much for their replacements. During her stay in Peru, Ida Shoatz (Philadelphia, Pa.) walked and rode horseback along the steep trails that lead through the mountains around the Indian town of Pisac. She managed a school lunch program in thirteen mountain villages under the auspices of the National School Feeding Plan.

A big part of Ida's job was to convince parents of the value of daily hot meals. Ancient superstitions and fears were a barrier. One Volunteer reported: "We are still trying to overcome antipathy toward milk. When we started, we mixed the milk powder in weak concentrations and then, as the children grew used to it, we built up the strength to its proper proportion. Nevertheless, we still hear that milk is not good for children, that it gives them stomach ache."

Irrigation canal in progress. Volunteer Michael Manetsch and two Indians from the village of Cuyo Chico stand in the deep slice they have carved through an enormous boulder. When completed, the canal will link with a mountain stream and carry enough water to irrigate 160 acres of land.

Manetsch works with the transit given by a Peruvian government agency.

Indian workers shovel broken rock while Mike Manetsch takes his turn on the portable jack hammer, which came from the Agency for International Development. The jack hammer dramatically increased the rate of digging the two-mile canal along the face of a mountain.

Ida lived at a school on the edge of Pisac with another Volunteer. Together they improvised fund-raising schemes. "We make doughnuts and popcorn and sell them on Sundays in the market place, mainly to tourists," she said while in Pisac. "We've made several hundred dollars which we'll use to send the kids to camp."

Ida was the first Negro ever to be seen in Pisac. "They thought it was most unusual for me to live with a white Volunteer," she said. "Now color doesn't make any difference. They've accepted us both with open arms."

Volunteers look with impatience and despair at the lack of tangible progress (a very few Volunteers have surrendered and returned home), but here and there dramatic achievements have been wrought. A good example is the digging of an irrigation canal under the guidance of Frank Billman (Akron, Ohio) and Michael Manetsch (Yakima, Wash.) to serve a community of farmers.

Manetsch, shown at work on the canal on these pages, came with five other Volunteers to Cuyo Chico, a high Andean hamlet of two hundred huts of adobe and thatch. The village is situated almost two

will be a boon to Cuyo Chico. It will mean that an additional 160 acres of land can be farmed and that the peasant cultivators can get two crops from their fields each year instead of one.

If every Peace Corps Volunteer could return to the United States with such an achievement behind him, optimism would run high in the Corps. Usually the Volunteer has to be satisfied with the hope that he has made an inch of progress, that he has been able to urge some forces into initial motion. Determination against immeasurable odds must replace North American impatience to get things done. But sometimes results come from unexpected sources. The Peruvian government, following America's example, has started a Peace Corps of its own—Cooperación Popular—which sends university students to the mountains on campaigns of self-help for the Indians.

Stopping to rest in a mountain village, Ida Shoatz partakes of a snack at a food vendor's table. Ida managed a school lunch program in thirteen villages near Pisac.

In Pisac's market Ida Shoatz shops for the ingredients of her evening meal. It is Sunday afternoon, the day the tourists come to town to see the Inca ruins in the area, hence the automobiles in the background.

miles above sea level. Ruins of an Inca fortress still guard the valley from above Cuyo Chico and the villagers still farm terraces made centuries ago by their ancestors.

Manetsch spent his first two months in the area building sheep-dip tanks for a neighboring village. Then he put to use the knowledge of surveying he had picked up in summer work for the Washington State Highway Department—he joined the farmers of Cuyo Chico in the backbreaking project they had begun three years earlier: digging a two-mile canal along the face of a mountain.

Much of the canal's path lay through solid rock, and the going had been painfully slow for the Indian farmers, who with their hand tools were digging about a foot and a half a day. Manetsch talked the United States Agency for International Development into giving the village a portable jack hammer; the Peruvian government supplied dynamite and a transit. Soon the ditch was being pushed ahead at the rate of sixteen feet a day. Having learned from Manetsch the use of the new equipment, the Indians are completing the canal on their own.

The water flowing through this canal

Chile

Chile, 2,650 miles long and nowhere more than 250 miles wide, can well boast of her natural beauty—a land of lakes, mountains, valleys, fertile farmlands—and of her cities, with broad boulevards, lofty office buildings, and balconied apartments. She can also be proud of her rich mineral deposits of copper and nitrates, which have made her standard of living one of the continent's highest. But Chile also carries a staggering burden of poverty and social dislocation, as evidenced by the slums surrounding her cities (a phenomenon repeated all over South America), to which Indians have come to live in *cayampas*, shelters made of cardboard, tin, and old tires.

Chile's population of over 8,000,000 forms a unique group among the Ameri-

Top, a farmer and his oxen come to the rescue of Emory Tomor, whose jeep has gotten stuck in the mire near Galvarino, an Araucanian Indian village in southern Chile.

Tomor, the first non-Indian ever to live in the Galvarino area, calls upon an Araucanian family gathered in the doorway of their thatched hut.

After unloading their grain, Indian farmers relax outside the warehouse of the food and grain co-op set up by Tomor in Galvarino.

can peoples. Chileans are chiefly of Spanish descent, and there are large groups of English, German, Slavic, Italian, and Irish in the national pool. Chile was conquered in the fifteenth century by Pedro de Valdivia who, instead of finding gold and silver, encountered an agricultural paradise peopled by the warlike Araucanian Indians. The Araucanians resisted all attempts of conquest by the Spanish and fought a magnificent battle against the invaders. The struggle ended only during the last century, at much the same time

that our own West was being tamed.

Because of a rapidly increasing population, these industrious and fiercely independent people find themselves wrestling with many social and economic problems. Each year thousands of villagers leave the back country and make their way to Santiago, the capital, and other large cities, hoping to find work. Instead, they find what nearly half a million *campesinos* in Santiago have already found: slums, misery, and lack of opportunities.

To effect critically needed changes, the government has spurred its social agencies to action in education, health, and community development. The Peace Corps

was called upon to assist in these projects under the aegis of such departments as the Social Services Agency of the Chilean Ministry, the Chilean Institute for Popular Education, and the Institute of Rural Education. In early 1965, the twelve groups of Volunteers in Chile were engaging in education, housing, social service work; conducting public health programs; helping to improve agricultural techniques; and developing cooperatives to improve the lot of the farmer and the city craftsman. Volunteers have made a good start in the formation of cooperatives. The experience of one Volunteer, Emory L. Tomor (Encino, Calif.), is a bright example.

During his first six months in Chile, Tomor taught in the Institute of Rural Education, where he pushed the idea of cooperatives. One day a student of his, Antonio Millape Caniuqueor, an Araucanian Indian, said to him, "Come and work with us. I have been telling my people about cooperatives for over a year. They will believe you more than me."

Tomor received his director's approval, and he went to live with three hundred Araucanian farmers and their families in

Below left, Tomor, wrapped in blanket, joins Araucanian farmers in a rest period during a fence-building job on one of their farms.

This Araucanian youth, wearing the headdress of an Indian ritual dance and a modern coat and shirt, symbolizes the convergence of two worlds.

the valley of Llufquentúe, which means "place of torments" in the Araucanian language. It was among these people that Tomor was to form the first small farmers' cooperative in the south of Chile.

Tomor overcame the Indians' suspiciousness by picking up Mapudumu, their dialect. They in turn learned snatches of English. He traveled about the countryside, getting acquainted with the farmers and their families. Presently, he was able to set up a food and grain cooperative in Galvarino, the valley town. Tomor built himself a house with the help of the Indians and it soon became the headquarters of the cooperative.

The farmers there are desperately poor. Before the co-op, they earned an average of only forty dollars a year, and they were forced to borrow capital at exorbitant rates from usurers. Through Tomor's co-op they could borrow at a straight 6 per cent. The co-op, which began with forty-five members, grew to include over two hundred farmers.

In addition to managing the co-op, Tomor worked with the Indians to build

Above, Araucanian farmers who joined Tomor's food and grain co-op.

Inside the co-op warehouse, Tomor, at table in center, goes over some paper work with the aid of several co-workers. Araucanian farmers drift in to get their quota of seed.

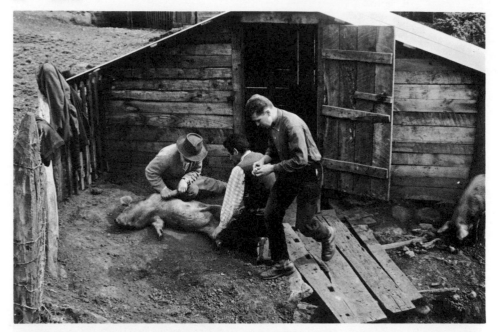

new access roads and bridges, which enabled them to get their produce to market faster.

After a while, Tomor realized that the cooperative alone was not sufficient. Something more had to be done to better the farmers' lot. Agricultural enterprises other than wheat growing would have to be started to increase their income.

Tomor knew some of the U. S. agricultural specialists who were working as advisers with the Chilean government. At his invitation, they investigated the situation and recommended an attempt at vegetable raising and adding poultry and hogs to the Araucanians' livestock.

The chief of the community in which Tomor lived and president of the cooperative, Manuel Paillal, felled some trees and, following a model Tomor had made, built a farrowing house for four sows. Fifteen other farmers followed the chief's example. Tomor helped to set their houses up. Working side by side with the farmers, he inoculated their pigs against disease. Until then, the Araucanians had been keeping dwarfed hogs that took two years to grow to market size, during which time they roamed over the fields doing more damage than the price they brought. To keep the animals close to home, Tomor advised the farmers to fell trees and split logs for fence posts on the farms.

At the end of his two-year tour in Chile Tomor applied for an extension. Later he wrote:

"Personally I had had enough of the Peace Corps. I still liked the idea of it and had a feeling of accomplishment. At the same time I had a sick feeling of having been let down somewhere along the line by the people back home whom I was representing in this forsaken part of the world. All of my fellow Volunteers who had, through the nature of our work, become more independent and individualistic than ever were headed home to work in the government, to be drafted by the Army, or to go back to school. It seemed that by our system back home none of us was fit for life. In view of this I could not very well afford to lose more time.

"At the same time I had enjoyed my

Top, with the help of two farmers, Tomor helps to inoculate a hog against disease.

In the woods near Galvarino, Tomor, left, and farmers cut eucalyptus logs, which will be split later for fence posts.

work more than anything I had done before, and certainly more than the above-mentioned possibilities. If the Peace Corps approved my extension, I was willing. They did. So I am staying with the people of the valley a while longer, preparing others to take over when I leave. When that day comes I hope to take with me some of their natural dignity and simple way of life."

Other cooperatives took hold in Chile, and they were started by Volunteers like Tomor. Lee Bettis (Winter Park, Fla.) and his wife, Lucille, a Philadelphia girl, who were married two months after they arrived in Chile, were assigned to Santiago. In La Victoria, a slum district of Santiago, Lee started a cobblers' cooperative. He had talked to local cobblers and learned that they were having difficulty obtaining leather at reasonable prices. Lee persuaded them that it would be to their advantage to buy their materials as a group. It was from these talks that the first cooperative of craftsmen in Santiago was formed.

Before Lee started the co-op, he and his

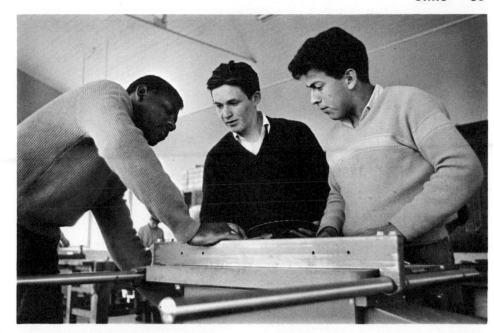

wife were expected to open a day-care center for the children of women workers in a trousers factory. To the Bettises' dismay, they found that the site for the nursery was being used as a garbage dump.

In a school near Osorno, a city in southern Chile, Wendell Gorum, left, instructs farm boys in carpentry.

Gorum joins his pupils for some entertainment by a guitar player.

With the help of other Volunteers and fathers in the neighborhood, they cleaned up the filth and built a lean-to to shelter the children. In time, the lean-to was replaced by a permanent building. Now forty youngsters come to the nursery every morning, and the center has a small library and a clinic run by a Peace Corps nurse.

Far afield from where Tomor and Bettis were developing their co-ops, Walter Harrison (Lombard, Ill.), a graduate of the University of Illinois, was starting one of his own, a ragpickers' co-op in Osorno, in southern Chile. Before his arrival the pickers were gleaning bones, glass, and metal from the town dump, which they sold to middlemen who pocketed most of the profit. Harrison went out to the dump and convinced the pickers to organize. The co-op now has

Lee Bettis talks to a cobbler in La Victoria, a slum district of Santiago. Lee set up a cobblers' cooperative in the district, and his wife, Lucille, began a day-care nursery.

The La Victoria cobbler and his family. The box on which the shoe rests is his workbench.

twenty members, both men and women. Their gleanings go directly to Santiago, by-passing the middlemen. Formerly they got thirty pesos per kilo for their bones; now as a co-op they get fifty. Observed Harrison at the time: "This is real basic economics. I've started at the bottom helping the people who need help most."

Many Volunteers in Chile are teachers who get involved in community development work and who promote cooperatives on the side. They are either working with the Institute for Rural Education or the Rural Life Foundation, or with the Y.W.C.A., in programs of youth education and recreation. They are all part of the larger organization, the Chilean Institute for Popular Education, which was founded in 1955 to combat Chile's social problems through child and adult education and through programs of community development.

The program operates through community centers in slum neighborhoods in the cities and in underdeveloped rural areas. It promotes educational activity. General courses cover many subjects,

from arithmetic, history, and geography to nutrition, child care, local information, folklore, and sports. Vocational training includes such subjects as electricity, industrial mechanics, driving, barbering, carpentry, plumbing, drafting, and metal-

At the day-care center, Lucille Bettis and her children play a version of musical chairs.

Lucille visits the pants factory where the mothers of the children work.

working. There are also courses in sewing, weaving, dressmaking, home economics, and cooking.

One of the Volunteers who assisted in this program was Wendell J. L. Gorum (Hickory, Va.). In a school near Osorno, he instructed farm boys in carpentry as part of the program to equip rural youths with skills that will enable them to leave the countryside to take jobs in the city. Gorum also ran the school's athletic program.

The Institute has had a great deal of success in developing its program. Beginning with only two seminars to train instructors, it has since grown to the point where in 1962 the program could offer 141 courses to more than six thousand students. But as the program grows, more teachers are needed, and that is where the Peace Corps is rendering an invaluable service.

Top, Osorno ragpickers go after the bottles, bones, and metal in the town dump, their only means of livelihood.

An Osorno ragpicker and his family.

Walter Harrison, below, center, organized the ragpickers into a co-op, enabling them to by-pass middlemen and increase their earnings. Here, he watches while members of the co-op weigh the day's take.

Ecuador

It was shortly after their arrival in Manta, a fishing port one degree south of the equator, that Rhoda and Earle Brooks, a Peace Corps Volunteer couple from Minneapolis, decided to live among the fisherfolk in Tarqui. Tarqui was a community about a mile south of Manta around the sandy bay shore, and only the poorer families lived there.

The Brookses picked out an old warehouse on the beach in Tarqui for their residence. While they were sweeping debris, including dozens of dead rats, from the two-room structure, a group of fishermen approached. The men watched in silence as Rhoda and Earle swept pile after pile of junk and filth through the doorway. At length, one of the older men spoke up. "Are you going to live *here?*" he asked.

When the Brookses affirmed this, he exclaimed that gringos lived in Manta, not along the beach among the fishermen. Earle Brooks replied that he and his wife were going to work in Manta, but they preferred to live there on the lovely beach near the blue ocean.

At that the fishermen smiled warmly and welcomed the young couple. Apparently the complimentary description of their neighborhood convinced them of what they had found hard to believe. One strapping fisherman stepped forward to offer his hand.

"My name is Mariano and these are my sons." He waved proudly toward a clutch of barefoot youngsters. "We will be glad to help you clean out your house," he grinned.

After the warehouse was emptied of rubbish, Mariano showed the Brookses how to clean the floors with wet sand and to wash the walls with a dry rag.

He explained that there was no source of fresh water in Manta. The Brookses would have to conserve the few barrels they could buy when the out-of-town water vendor came around with his burros each week.

Having only their subsistence allowances to draw from, Rhoda and Earle were forced to use simple materials in fashioning the warehouse into a comfortable place to live. They built chairs from bamboo, a desk and table from rough boards, and lamps from chicken wire and

paper. They installed a waterless kitchen in a hallway, bought a kerosene stove, and borrowed a bed. They even built a fenced-in, gravel-floored patio to relax in during their few leisure hours. The warehouse was to be their home for nearly two years.

Word of the Volunteers' renovation project spread all the way back to Manta. Soon curious visitors began to appear. One Sunday afternoon the Brookses found themselves playing host to over

Rhoda Brooks is followed by a cluster of children in the port town of Manta as she starts out on one of her morning rounds to encourage women to come to her homemaking classes.

forty uninvited guests. Rhoda hastily prepared a fruit punch. Housewives marveled over the furniture, the tasteful decorations, and the compact kitchen. They couldn't believe that the Brookses had done all this without servants.

Gulls fill the air over the beach at Tarqui, near Manta. From their home, Rhoda and Earle Brooks had an unobstructed view of the sea, the fishermen, and their craft. The hollowed-out log canoe, at right, is called a bongo.

In her front yard, Rhoda teaches neighborhood women how to make banana bread.

"You gringos have such good ideas—you know how to do everything," one lady remarked. "But we can't. It's just impossible for us."

It was precisely this attitude, and the conditions it perpetuates, that the Brookses, community development workers, sought to correct. Most of Manta's 40,000 people are poor and live in squalor. In some *barrios* (districts) Earle Brooks saw, garbage was allowed to pile up in the streets and under the stilt foundations of houses. The people disliked living amidst heaps of rubbish and suspected that it bred disease, but no one seemed inclined to do anything about it. Somebody else, some other day, would clean it up.

For their first community development experiment, Rhoda and Earle called a meeting in a *barrio* household to discuss the problems in the district. The lady of the house introduced them to the assemblage. "These are our friends, *Voluntarios del Cuerpo de Paz.* They are here to help us improve our *barrio.*"

"We need a bulldozer and an automatic garbage collector to clean our streets," one man interjected.

"We don't have equipment to give you," Earle explained. "But we can help you find ways to clean up your *barrio* if you really want to work on it yourselves."

By the end of the meeting many problems had come under discussion, but all agreed that removing the garbage was most urgent. Earle and the men laid out a

plan of action. The following Saturday morning a group would gather for a rake-making session. Earle would ask the city to lend the *barrio* a truck on Sunday (the city cooperated). On Saturday night the Volunteers would show a movie—a Walt Disney film depicting the life cycle of flies, how they lay eggs in garbage, and how they spread disease—in a *barrio* street to arouse interest. On Sunday the *minga*, or cleanup, itself would take place.

Everything went according to schedule, and by nightfall Sunday, after young and old had pitched in, scrambling for the rakes and filling the truck five times, the streets were spotless. That evening the men discussed plans for using garbage cans in the future and making regular collections.

Thus, the Brookses' first attempt was a heartwarming success. At the end of their twenty-month hitch in Manta they could

Rhoda visits a Manta school, one of several in which she helped to install brick ovens for cooking hot lunches.

Rhoda and Earle Brooks relax for a brief spell on the patio of their seaside home. Listening attentively to Rhoda's guitar playing is little Koki, a neighborhood child, whom they later adopted.

Volunteer Martha Seymour (New York City) stops to chat with a neighbor in Cerro Santa Ana. She talked one hundred women into attending her homemaking classes and ran a summer camp for children.

Below left, Martha gets a grand welcome by youngsters as she passes their house on one of her rounds in the Cerro Santa Ana barrio (district) of Guayaquil, Ecuador's largest city and principal port, where she was a community development worker.

Barbara Tetrault (Hopewell Junction, N. Y.) shows a class of young artists how to draw a rooster, in Guayaquil.

look back on many other achievements: hot school-lunch programs; classes in nutrition, child care, carpentry, and mechanics; and the first swimming lessons ever taught in Manta.

Friends in Manta and Tarqui lamented the Volunteers' departure. Rhoda and Earle adopted two bright youngsters, Koki, aged three, and Carmen, two, and brought them back to the United States.

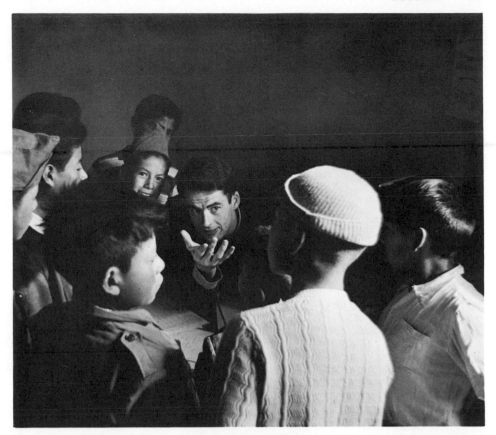

When the city government of Quito, Ecuador's capital, ordered the betuneros, or shoeshine urchins, off the main plaza because of their ragamuffin appearance, Sam McPhetres (Juneau, Alaska) organized the boys, got them neat uniforms, and, from a rented two-room headquarters in the center of the city, dispatched them each morning to assigned positions, including the plaza. Before they got their uniforms, the boys received forty centavos (two cents) per shine; now they earn sixty centavos.

Robert Griffen (Los Angeles) and his wife, Florence, traveled around rural Ecuador giving public health lessons, which were illustrated with cartoons—as they are doing here in Quinche, a village near Quito. Griffen has just drawn a disease-carrying germ. Mrs. Griffen holds his paper in place.

Venezuela

The economic statistics of Venezuela compare favorably with those of her brother and sister nations. Budget surpluses, mounting foreign reserves, and a per capita income of $900—the highest in Latin America—make her the envy of the continent. Oil, as all the world knows, is the source of her wealth, and within the past ten years she has also begun to extract rich deposits of iron ore and more recently to make her own steel.

What are the social and economic problems in Venezuela? Poverty, slums. Simmering antidemocratic forces. The country's great natural wealth has not gotten a very wide distribution, although a significantly large middle class exists and is growing. An almost barbarously tempestuous political cavalcade has in the past kept social and economic opportunity out of reach for most people. Since 1959, however, and the election of Rómulo Betan-

Top, in a Caracas slum, Volunteer Jerry Page, a recreation director, is surrounded by boys who want him to play baseball. The time is during the Cuban missile crisis of 1962, when many anti-American slogans were daubed on walls. This one exclaims, "Away with Kennedy."

Winning and keeping the boys' trust often depended upon something as simple as a Yo-yo. Jerry Page gave demonstrations and kept his young charges supplied with strings.

court to the Presidency and the transferral of that office in 1964 to Raúl Leoni through honest and free elections—successfully conducted in the face of terrorist threats—Venezuelan politics has made a historic adjustment that promises well for the future.

Anti-American sentiment intermittently flashes through the squatter slums around Caracas. During the Cuban missile crisis of 1962, Volunteer Jerry Page (Denver, Colo.), a Peace Corps recreation director, was on his way to visit a friend in Las Tunitas—a Caracas slum not far from where the Nixons were attacked in 1958—when he was besieged by a band of cheering, idolizing youngsters. They were members of his recreation program and

Jerry Page umpires a game on the new playground that he, his boys, and neighborhood fathers landscaped.

A bloque *family poses with a Peace Corps Volunteer. Jerry Page was often invited to Sunday dinner by the boys in his recreation program.* Bloques *are giant apartment buildings erected to provide housing for the poor and to clear shantytowns.*

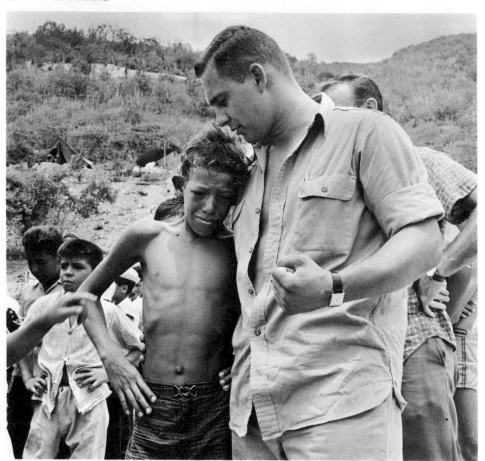

wanted him to play ball. They fell in behind Jerry and followed him. The group passed a wall bearing a painted slogan: *Fuera Kennedy* ("Away with Kennedy"). The boys seemed to take no notice of it.

The fact is that Peace Corps Volunteers in Caracas slums have succeeded where others have failed; they have overcome the coldness and deep mistrust usually shown to North Americans there. One American worked for seventeen years with the people of Catia, the district in which Jerry Page lived, and was not once invited into a home; but nearly every Sunday one of Jerry Page's boys took him home for dinner. As for the anti-American slogans, a slum dweller pointed to one that had been scrawled on a wall and ex-

Dan Gadra (Buffalo, N. Y.) gives heart to a boy reluctant to go back home on his last day at camp. Gadra and two other Volunteers built the camp for the boys of Las Tunitas, one of Caracas' worst slums.

The signal to start a rousing tug of war, umpired by Dan Gadra, on a playground in Las Tunitas. Before the Volunteers went to Caracas, these children had nothing to do but roam the streets.

plained, "This mean Yankee go home, not Peace Corps."

When Jerry Page first moved into Catia, he found no playground, no sports equipment, no recreational facilities or supervision whatsoever. For five years local officials had been promising a baseball diamond to the community. With a little initiative and resourcefulness from Page, construction of the diamond was soon under way. He recruited the help of nearly every boy and many adults in the community to landscape the playground out of a hillside in adjacent Las Tunitas.

Now the boys in Catia at least have a few square yards of open space in which to play ball, and they also have their first experience with rules and umpires. "They

An exhortation to try again from Jerome Reinisch (Bronx, N. Y.). Reinisch and two other Volunteers ran a flourishing Y.M.C.A. recreation program in Puerto Cabello, a seaport west of Caracas.

In Rubio, a town near the Colombian border, Harriette Osborn (Kadoka, S. D.), fifty-two, explains a game to fascinated farm girls. Mrs. Osborn, a widow, was an agriculture extension agent in southwestern Venezuela.

haven't the slightest idea of what sportsmanship means," said Page of his boys. "If they don't like what's going on during a game they walk off the field. They fight with each other and with the umpire. I want them to get to the point where they will stick the game out and respect the other players and the authority of the umpire."

Because of her burgeoning population, Venezuela has a disproportionately large number of young people and it is they who need attention most. Jerry Page's playground is just one example among many Peace Corps projects in Venezuelan cities, most of which were developed under Y.M.C.A. auspices.

Venezuela possesses modern cities, providing prosperity for some and the promise of it for others; she also has the primitive Orinoco River, and jungles, broad plains, and mountains. Some parts of Venezuela are so wild that civilized men fear to penetrate them. But in the provinces lives a large segment of Venezuelans depending chiefly on the land for a livelihood. As in other Latin American countries, the people of the hinterlands exert pressure on the cities by migrating to them.

With the emphasis again on youth, the Venezuelan government is offering hope and stimulation to its rural people. The Peace Corps helps. Volunteers have organized 5-V clubs, patterned after the 4-H movement in the United States. A multitude of skills are being taught, among them beekeeping, poultry- and rabbit-raising, carpentry, cooking, and sewing.

The government hopes that the 5-V programs will spread homemaking and agricultural skills and raise the standard of living in the rural areas. Unless something is done to make country life more attractive, the crushing migration to the cities will go on. The population of Caracas, which in 1950 was estimated at 376,000, had grown to 1,300,000 by 1962.

Top, in San Cristóbal, an agricultural center, Mrs. Hazel Pell (Barrington, Ill.), fifty, teaches carpentry to a class of girls. It is the woman who is expected to handle tools, not the man, in Venezuela. Mrs. Pell and her husband, Charles, fifty-two, taught homemaking and agricultural skills to farm children.

A group of youngsters learns how to graft a citrus tree from Michael L. Peters (Grundy Center, Iowa) in the mountain town of Santa Ana.

Brazil

"There are more sounds which aggravate, smells which nauseate, sights which irritate. Sewage runs down the hill from one house past another, children running barefoot through it."

This is a Peace Corps doctor's description of the *favelas*, or hillside slums, of glamorous Rio de Janeiro.

"Garbage accumulates in the sun. Pregnant women daily climb the hill with cans of water on their heads. Food, water (usually unsafe), and medical care must be procured below."

Compared to those in other South American cities, Rio's slums are old and familiar (the movie *Black Orpheus*, viewed

Top, the favelas, *or hillside slums, that ring Rio de Janerio.*

A Rio favela *family stands outside its flimsy shack.*

Linda Mathieson (Phoenix, Ariz.), a social worker, talks to favela mothers waiting to have their babies examined inside a clinic in Rio.

A favela mother and child at the clinic.

by millions around the world, was set in Rio's *favelas*) and in the carnival city *par excellence* poverty is deep and disease commonplace. For every two babies born, one dies in infancy.

Rio and its environs make up the State of Guanabara, which maintains a network of free hospitals and health posts for its citizens. A shortage of personnel, however, limits the amount of medical services that can be provided. Peace Corps Volunteers have been asked to relieve the shortage by filling staff positions and training Brazilians in the medical arts. The Volunteers fall into several categories: *Visitadoras*, or visiting health educators; X-ray technicians; registered nurses; and *Guardas Sanitarios*, or health educators specializing in sanitation.

Besides the Volunteers involved in Rio's health programs, others are scattered throughout Brazil participating in rural and urban community development, education, agriculture, and school lunch programs.

Volunteers skilled in agriculture are encouraging farmers to plant diverse crops, for Brazil's economy, heavily dependent upon huge coffee exports, suffers violent reactions from fluctuations in world coffee prices. Volunteer agriculturists also assist in the growth of 4-H clubs, demonstrate simple fertilization techniques, and help plan and construct small earth dams to store water.

Malnutrition, caused by an outright lack of food or by deficient traditional diets, is encountered frequently. The Brazilian government is trying to raise nutrition standards by furnishing one free meal a day to its school children. Food for Peace is cooperating by supplying the food, and Peace Corps Volunteers are helping to administer the program.

A young Rio patient, clinging to her doll, gets reassurance from nurse Theresa Ricks (Hollis, N. Y.) that the medicine will benefit her.

Below right, nurse Marietta Struchen (Rupert, Ida.) prepares to administer a shot to a favela *patient in a Rio hospital.*

Nurse Nancy Conway (Foxboro, Mass.) puts a young patient on the scales in a Rio hospital.

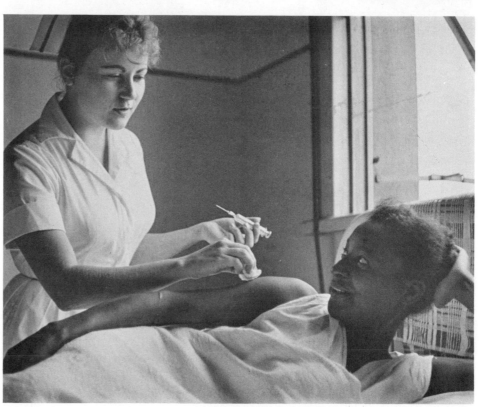

El Salvador

A young man from Coraopolis, Pennsylvania, has left a deep mark on Tonacatepeque, a rural town of about eight thousand people in El Salvador. His name is James J. Portman, and he went to the smallest Central American republic on May 3, 1962, with twenty-three other Peace Corps Volunteers to take part in a community development program.

With her 2,500,000 people, El Salvador has one of the highest population densities in the Western Hemisphere. About two thirds of the Salvadorians reside in economically stagnant rural areas haphazardly taking a living from the soil. Most of the men who call themselves farmers own only small plots of land and are hampered by primitive methods of cultivation. Motivation for self-improvement is low, and the farmer and his family are apt to suffer from malnutrition. One of the sad effects of insufficient nourishment is a high infant mortality rate: the rate in El Salvador is nearly forty times that in the United States.

The only Volunteer assigned to the town of Tonacatepeque, reputed to be the poorest town of all in an impoverished country, James Portman selected a group of boys there and asked them to keep a record of the foods they ate for one week. He found out that only one in eight had eaten meat, and that only a few had eaten eggs. Their diet consisted of little besides beans, rice, *tortillas*, and coffee. Portman decided to spend his initial efforts in teaching the fundamentals of good nutrition. He also planned to show the villagers how they might obtain for themselves the foods that they lacked.

To give them a start, he bought one hundred ducklings and three hundred chicks, out of his own pocket money, from suppliers in the United States. With this healthy stock, he taught the two hundred boys in his 4-H club how to care for, feed, kill, and dress poultry. Eggs produced by the mature birds were hatched in an incubator supplied by the Peace Corps and, as the chickens and ducks multiplied, they were distributed among the boys to raise on their own. Be-

With proper care, ducklings and chicks grow, lay eggs, and multiply. The 4-H club boys of Tonacatepeque learn from James Portman two phases of successful poultry raising.

As Portman heads for his jeep, children begin to gather around, hoping for a ride.

A trip to an outlying farm means a capacity load for Portman's Peace Corps jeep.

fore Portman left El Salvador for the United States, eggs and poultry in Tonacatepeque were abundant, and the diets of many families had been substantially improved.

Fresh vegetables were also in short supply when Portman arrived in the town. To remedy the shortage he came up with the simple solution of instructing his boys to plant vegetable gardens at home. And with their help, Portman planted a huge demonstration garden next to the town's church. Soon there were enough vegetables for the entire village, and even a small surplus, which was sold in neighboring towns. Portman destroyed the myth that gardening had to be limited to the six wet months of the year. When local farmers predicted that he couldn't raise a second crop of vegetables after the wet season, he introduced them to the technique of moisture preservation by mulching and harvested a bumper crop of vegetables. In another demonstration project,

Portman took ten small farms on the town's edge where crops had been planted in a hit-or-miss fashion and where the soil was eroding away. He worked patiently with the farmers, showing them how to diversify their crops and how to plant them on a contour to check the erosion. The increased yields brought about by these measures meant that the farmers earned several hundred dollars extra the very first year—an enormous sum to them.

Portman immersed himself in the life of Tonacatepeque. He practiced self-denial to perhaps an extreme degree, spending a large part of his subsistence allowance on the many projects he initiated. He worked hard, ate little, and lost weight. A Catholic, he maintained an active interest in the community's church, to which he contributed generously. Portman and the parish priest, Father Daniel Martinez, were close friends and worked effectively together in bringing people back to the church, which had become something of an anachronism. Economic inertia had deadened the town's spiritual life as well as its agriculture and only a smattering of worshippers were in the habit of going to church, but Portman attended Mass every Sunday. Because he was so well liked and was looked upon as a leader, the villagers soon followed his example and the church enjoyed a renaissance.

Poverty's hypnotic effects had settled over the town's domestic industries, too. An adult male, by picking up odd jobs, *could* work twelve hours—for a wage of thirty cents—but the standards by which we measure employment in the United States were hardly applicable in Tonacatepeque. A clothing industry had at one time thrived there and a few women were still engaged in the trade on a small scale in their homes. Portman thought it was possible to revive this industry and he persuaded a New York relief agency to send him two sewing machines and five hundred yards of cloth. With this equipment as a beginning, he set up a sewing

Top, Mass lets out on a Sunday morning in Tonacatepeque. Church attendance increased while James Portman was there and the parish regained its position as a cohesive influence in the community.

Standing in the demonstration garden he planted next to the church, Portman talks to Father Daniel Martinez. Together they made an energetic team.

class for his girls' club. As a boy, Portman had watched his grandmother make braided rugs from scrap cloth, and as a student at Pennsylvania State he had successfully used the rug designs in his extension work with the Amish. Portman taught this art to the women and girls of Tonacatepeque so that they might increase family incomes by making and selling rugs.

In another enterprise, Portman had his boys plant flowers with seed donated by an American seed producer. They planted them all over town—in front of their homes, in the park and market place, in the churchyard, wherever there was an open space. They let the flowers go to seed and the seeds were gathered up and packaged. In a lively selling campaign the boys sold out their stock in a few days at two cents a packet.

These may seem like insignificant achievements—and there were many others like them—but if a family increased its income by fifty cents a day it meant a doubling or tripling of what it had made before. Portman continually searched for new ways of showing the villagers how they could help themselves by utilizing the simple materials and resources they already possessed.

Portman became a cynosure in the town. Wherever he went, a trail of youngsters followed in Pied Piper fashion. He put in a long day, rising at 5 A.M. and dropping into bed exhausted at 10:30 in the evening. His rented room over a dry-goods store was cluttered with the paraphernalia of a greenhouse, a workshop, a library (sample titles: *Field Crop Insects*, *Growing Fruit and Vegetable Crops*), and a laboratory. Plant seedlings in wooden boxes grew among paint cans and tools. Dr. Salisbury's Poultry Disease Chart hung over his cot. He was denied privacy except when he slept, since visitors filed in and out of his room whenever he was there.

The too-often-repeated "ambassador of good will" label certainly applied with

Top, a cheerful vendor offers wares from her kitchen to "Hymie," as Portman was called.

Portman speaks to a woman who helps support her family by making shirts. At one time there had been a thriving cottage-type clothing industry in Tonacatepeque, but lower-priced imports and textile plants closer to El Salvador's capital had destroyed the town's ability to compete.

Portman, trailed by Tonacatepeque's worshipping youngsters.
The antidote to tropical heat: coconut milk. Here Portman and a farmer's son quench their thirst. Portman had stopped at the farm during a hot afternoon. To offer refreshment to his guest, the farmer promptly scaled a tree, knocked down a few coconuts, and hacked them open with his machete.

force in Portman's case, but only in terms of results: he had more of the selfless teacher in him than the cunning ambassador. He won the full confidence and affection of Tonacatepeque, especially of its youngsters, by his genuine concern. He couldn't take a ride in his Peace Corps jeep without a load of passengers going along, eager to help him on his mission and to learn. When he first arrived, Portman told the townspeople that "Jim" would be too hard to pronounce and that they could call him "Jaime," which became "Hymie." Tonacatepeque knew little peace when James Portman was there and happy children jumped and pranced around him shouting, "Hymie! Hymie!"

Dominican Republic

One Sunday in the summer of 1962 a Peace Corps jeep drove into a remote mountain village in the north of the Dominican Republic. So distantly isolated was the village that its people hadn't seen an American since the end of the U. S. Marine occupation of the country in 1924. The Volunteers had to do a lot of talking. They had to convince the astounded villagers that they indeed were not Marines.

Misidentification was one problem that Jess Stone (Englewood, Colo.) and Bennie Barela (Las Cruces, N. M.) didn't have to contend with. They were assigned to the comparatively large farming town of

Top, Bennie Barela, center, and Jess Stone, right, talk with a local official of the agriculture extension service in Baní. Somebody had painted a slogan—"Away with reaction, down with the Yankees"—outside his door.

In front of a grocery store a school kitchen comes under discussion. Stone, right, leaning forward, tries to get support for the idea.

Baní (population 14,000) in the south, about thirty miles west of the capital city, Santo Domingo. Using Baní as their center of operations, they traveled frequently to the outlying communities in the area.

On one routine afternoon, Jess maneuvered his jeep along a dusty, rutted road until he came to a village he and Bennie had visited some weeks before. They had planted the idea of adding a kitchen to the village school and Jess was now investigating to see if it had taken root.

His first stop in the village was the house of the headman, or mayor. Stone was received hospitably and offered a chair. When he began to review the school kitchen project and discuss its advantages, the mayor stubbornly shook his head and insisted that the village was too poor to undertake any such project.

"This," Stone relates, "is the standard reaction to any request from the outside for money. It is a reflex action left over from the days of the dictatorship."

The Volunteer strolled down to the village's only store, where a group of men were idling away the hot afternoon. Stone drew up a chair and started a conversation in his imperfect Spanish. He gossiped with the men for about an hour and then warily broached the subject of the school kitchen. The men were not particularly interested.

When school let out, the American approached the local version of the P.T.A. Some of the mothers indicated a desire to install the kitchen. But Stone was not encouraged. He knew that it would take several more meetings and probably some concrete demonstration of good will on his part and Barela's to muster enough support for the kitchen.

This experience was repeated many times; nonchalance prevailed around the Dominican countryside. Farmers looked askance at suggestions to change their antiquated methods of cultivating the soil. All the people were suspicious of government interest in their affairs after three decades of Rafael Trujillo's secret police dictatorship.

Broad agricultural reform is needed in the Dominican Republic. The country suf-

Top, with a test kit, Bennie Barela shows the members of a 4-H club how to test the soil in their school garden.

Jess Stone has a word with a farmer plowing his field. The farmer's son guides the plow horse.

fers from a common malady: a one-crop economy. Seventy per cent of the national income derives from sugar cane. The government wants to induce the farmers to diversify their crops and adopt modern farming techniques, but old habits are hard to change.

Hope for change lies with the country's youth, and for that reason Stone and Barela organized 4-H clubs and worked diligently with them. The Volunteers encouraged their club members to raise chickens and plant school vegetable gardens and proposed better methods of irrigation, the use of hybrid seeds, and the systematic use of fertilizers.

Peace Corps Volunteers have become a familiar sight in the Dominican rural areas. Nathan B. Witham (Newcastle, Me.) and Dale R. Martin (Long Creek, Ore.) worked out of San Juan, a farming center in the western part of the country. They, too, promoted the organization of 4-H clubs. They trained the leaders of their clubs thoroughly enough to start clubs themselves. In this way the clubs are proliferating.

Harvey Hartley (North Lima, Ohio) and Robert Williams (Framingham, Mass.) applied a typical community development technique to generate self-help in one tiny village that had two small, cottage-type industries. One group of women made mats and baskets out of woven grass. Another group made clay waterpots. Despite this earning potential, the village was hungry; the mats and pots were sold for a pittance to sharp-talking middlemen, who in turn sold them for great profit in the capital.

Didn't the women know they were being cheated? Why didn't they take their products to the city themselves? How much would a used truck cost? During a visit to the village Hartley and Williams spread these questions among the women for about an hour and then left them when they saw that the discussion was generating its own momentum. The Volunteers would return another day to see if any decisions had been reached.

Top, Dale Martin, rear, and Nate Witham, right, interrupt rice harvesters to ask them some questions.

Robert Williams talks to a group of women who carry on a small cottage-type industry in their village. They make woven baskets and clay pots, which are sold in Santo Domingo.

No one can measure the permanence of the Peace Corp's impression on the Dominican Republic. As the "third generation" of Volunteers goes to work there, hope is tempered with patience. But among the thousands of anecdotes which circulate among the Dominican Volunteers, the following stands out.

A village meeting was called after a report from the government that the

Sudden shower threatens to melt adobe bricks made by community development Volunteers experimenting with building materials new to their area. They are, from left to right, Vernon Guilliams (Butterfield, Minn.), Hill Phillips (Hinesville, Ga.), and John Greenough (Fort Smith, Ark.).

Below left, deep in the countryside, Volunteers Marion Ford (Paris, Tex.), left, and Bernard Isaacson (Brooklyn, N. Y.) look over a farmer's sick chicken. They had to admit they were stumped and said they would get an expert from the agriculture extension office to come out the next day.

Jess Stone gives a hand to two farmers who are building a chicken coop.

village's two Volunteers were going to be transferred to another site. A villager stood up and told the government's representative, "There have never been civic disturbances in this area, but if you take away our friends, there will be the damnedest riots you have ever seen."

At this point the local priest stood up and added, "And if there is a riot, I'll lead it."

The Volunteers stayed.

A proud father shows his newest offspring to Mike Dillon (West Palm Beach, Fla.), right, and Charles Loughran (Pittsburgh, Pa.) during a visit to his village.

Friendly meeting. Two youngsters are greeted by Harvey Hartley, a community development worker. Harvey was killed in an automobile accident shortly before returning to the United States.

Marion Ford talks with a farmer who had a well in need of deepening and cleaning. The shortage of good drinking water is a chronic problem in many rural areas in the Dominican Republic.

British Honduras

On January 1, 1964, British Honduras, a Central American country about half the size of Switzerland, took an important step toward independence from the United Kingdom: the government was modified to give more power to local officials elected by the people. In a March, 1965, national election, British Honduras voted for a speed-up in the decolonization process. As the day of independence nears, however, greater local responsibility will have to be assumed for developing the country's human and material resources.

The material resources possessed by British Honduras are chicle and cedar—already exploited and exported in quantity—tropical forests of mahogany and pine, undiversified and undeveloped farmlands, and the waters of the Caribbean. Full utilization of these resources awaits technological advance, which in turn awaits a trained and educated citizenry. Ethnically, the country is composed of a mixture of stocks living in harmony. In a population of over 90,000, about 60 per cent of the people are mestizos and English-speaking Negroes. Mayas and Caribs are the two dominant Indian groups, and a sprinkling of Syrians, Chinese, and German Mennonites make up tiny minorities.

On October 30, 1961, British Honduras suffered a blow that nearly wrecked her prospects for economic advancement, drowned her capital, Belize, and certainly delayed her preparations for independence. The blow came out of the Caribbean, and it was called Hurricane Hattie. With winds gusting up to two hundred miles per hour, the hurricane smashed into British Honduras and swept across Belize, across other towns and villages, across the great mahogany and pine forests. Giant trees were uprooted and broken to bits. Tides kicked up by the storm inundated Belize with nine feet of water.

The storm left British Honduras in a state of utter devastation. Belize resembled a mud swamp. Fortunately, early warn-

---

Top, Taeko and Erwin Wong, a husband-and-wife team from Honolulu, visit a class of Maya Indian children in the rural community of San Antonio.

Mrs. Wong gives a lesson in weaving the pandanus fiber to some women in Punta Gorda.

ings allowed time for evacuation and fewer than 275 lives were lost. Damage to property, agriculture, commerce, and industry was estimated at $40 million. When compared to the country's gross national product of $26 million, the magnitude of the disaster becomes apparent.

As so often happens in the aftermath of natural disasters, British Hondurans have rallied together to rebuild their country with a new spirit of unity. The United States and the United Kingdom have given special funds to help recovery. Plans have been laid to build a new capital city fifty miles inland.

"Upon the Education of Its People the Fate of This Country Depends." Thus reads a motto that British Honduran officials prepared for display in classrooms throughout the country. It indicates an enlightened approach to preparation for independence. Creating an educated body of citizens and technicians will not only hasten the day of full self-government but it will insure stability and growth and true independence afterwards. No matter how amicably colonial powers have withdrawn from their colonies, much too often they have left a vacuum behind—in politics, education, agriculture, and industry. In a rush to gain full independence, the former colony is left more dependent than ever on outside assistance.

The need for teachers is most acute. There are many elementary schools in the country, but three fourths of the teachers have had only a primary education themselves. Before education in British Honduras can have any significance, teachers must be trained, and such training is being provided in part today by Peace Corps Volunteers.

The first group of thirty-three Volunteers arrived in September, 1962, and most of them were teachers or teacher trainers. Among that delegation was a married couple, Mr. and Mrs. Erwin Wong (Honolulu). Mr. Wong, then fifty-five, was an elementary school principal and his wife, Taeko, then forty-nine, was an elementary school teacher—both on leave

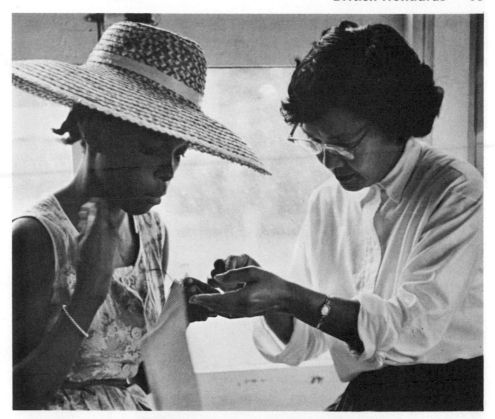

Top, when Mrs. Wong started her sewing class she had no material, so she cut the hems off several of her dresses. Here she helps a girl to master a stitch.

A warm greeting. Mr. Wong clasps a child's hand at one of the rural schools he and his wife visited near Punta Gorda.

Far left, the Wongs climb a hill toward a typical Maya home. They had had to go on foot to visit a school and were returning to their jeep parked on the other side of the hill.

Left, Mrs. Wong teaches a group of Maya youngsters a song in English.

From their house on the beach in Punta Gorda, the Wongs could see fishermen put out to sea each morning in their dugout canoes and return each evening with the catch. For the Wongs, like the villagers, fish was often the main meal. Bottom left, Mrs. Wong waits for a fisherman to reach shore in his canoe. Bottom right, coming ashore, the fisherman, wearing a battered hat and tattered shirt, hands over part of his catch. Right, Mrs. Wong delights in her purchase for the evening meal.

from the Honolulu public school system. They were assigned to Punta Gorda, a fishing town of about 1,800 people on the isolated southern coast of the country, not far from the Guatemalan border. Using Punta Gorda as their place of residence and base of operations, they went out into the surrounding countryside visiting rural schools. They traveled by jeep and sometimes by dugout canoe.

One of their regular stops was San Antonio, a Maya village eighteen miles away, at the end of the only road leading from Punta Gorda.

On one typical day, their jeep stopped in front of San Antonio's school. When the Wongs entered, they found classes in session. In one corner, a class was reciting a geography lesson; in another, a group of younger children was seated at a long table carefully copying addition problems from a blackboard. These children were black-haired, brown-eyed descendants of the Maya people, whose civilization flourished in Central America from 200 A.D. until the Spanish conquests. After a few minutes, the geography teacher took Mr. Wong aside.

"Mr. Wong, can you help me a little with longitude and latitude?" he asked. "I find the explanation a bit difficult."

"Certainly," Mr. Wong replied. "I can do it for you two ways. I can wait until after school or I can conduct the class a few minutes for you right now."

"*That* would be good. I'll be one of the students, too," he said enthusiastically.

For the next half-hour Mr. Wong used a small globe to unravel the mysteries of latitude and longitude for the attentive class.

While Mr. Wong was thus occupied,

Mrs. Wong slipped out to the jeep and came back with a long rapier-shaped leaf. After her husband finished his lesson, she held up the green and yellow leaf so that the children could see it.

"Do any of you know where there are plants growing with leaves like this?" she asked. A few hands tentatively went up.

"Its name is *pandanus*. If you find any, please bring them to school for me." She stripped a long fiber from the edge of the leaf. "You see, with this I can show your mothers how to make baskets and hats."

Skilled in the craft of weaving, many Punta Gorda women had long carried on an active business by sending their woven

Rosemary Marek takes her girls for a romp in the playground of a girl's school in Belize.

June Reed, at sixty-nine one of the oldest Volunteers in the Peace Corps, conducts an English class. "I've always been busy and I don't want to stop now," she said while teaching in Belize. "I want to be able to use what talents I have to help other people."

hats to Belize. But their profits had always been quite low because they used an inferior straw imported at considerable expense from Guatemala. (Using the imported fiber, it took a woman five days to weave a hat that sold in Belize for $1.50.)

Mrs. Wong was familiar with the excellent properties of the pandanus plant for making woven products, having used it to good advantage in her handicraft classes in Hawaii. Not knowing whether the plant was native to British Honduras at all, Mrs. Wong had searched sedulously until she found some growing on a beach. She had gathered a supply of leaves, cured them, and stripped them of their fibers. Then she had demonstrated to the delighted Punta Gorda women how easily it could be woven and taught them new

Edwin Voirol doubled as teacher and coach in a Belize girls' school. Here he readies a typing class for a speed test.

Rhubarb. Voirol arbitrates a dispute on the softball field, where he coached a men's team on his free afternoons. The young men were accustomed to playing a freewheeling, ruleless game.

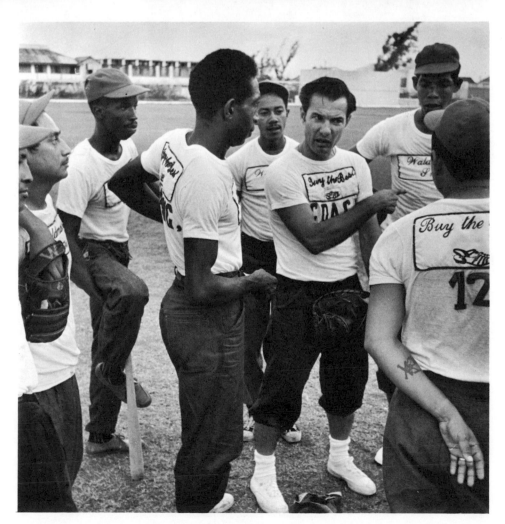

designs. In a short time they were making handbags, mats, and coasters as well as hats. Mrs. Wong was hoping that the pandanus also grew near San Antonio.

In such activities as this—modest to most Americans—the Wongs helped the people of the Punta Gorda area, inside school and out. Mrs. Wong conducted sewing classes for girls and taught them to make their own clothing. Outside their white frame house just at the sea's edge, the Wongs planted a vegetable garden to set an example for their neighbors. Vegetables were missing from the local diet because they had to be imported (or so it was believed) and were expensive. The Wongs showed that nothing prevented the Punta Gordans from growing their own vegetables.

Before they left, the Wongs were assigned to other sections of British Honduras. As always, they stressed improvement of the overall education of children,

but they also placed special emphasis on arts and crafts and developing skills that would have immediate practical value to students. The response of British Honduran education officials to their work was laudatory. One official went so far as to credit them with causing "the beginning of a revolution in our primary schools."

While the teacher trainers and a few community action workers covered the rural areas, in Belize Volunteer teachers had taken charge of many classes in primary, secondary, and technical schools. They taught English, science, chemistry, biology, mathematics, metalworking, physical education, shorthand, typing, and bookkeeping. In many cases, their assumption of teaching assignments allowed the regular Honduran teachers to pursue further education. The under-education of teachers in British Honduras was so extreme that when the plane carrying the original contingent of Volunteers touched down in Belize, the number of people holding university degrees in the country was more than doubled.

Rosemary Marek (Cadott, Wis.), an energetic blonde, taught physical education in seven secondary schools in hot, steamy Belize. She introduced competitive games to a curriculum which had previously offered only calisthenics. While she was there, she trained the Honduran physical education teachers to carry on the game program after she left.

Retired from a long teaching career that included setting up schools for Alaskan Eskimos in the early 1920's, June S. Reed (Coos Bay, Ore.) taught English at a Belize girls' school.

"The real need in this country," she said, "is getting people to speak English properly, since it is the official language. It is a problem, as the country is such a racial and cultural mixture with Spanish, Carib, Creole, Mayan, British, and American all being spoken and making their influences felt.

"The result of all this," she continued, "is a jargon which parents of our girls, and often their teachers, can't understand.

Top, in the heart of Belize, Volunteers join members of the city's police force in a game of volleyball. The Union Jack flies overhead.

With newly acquired skill, a British Honduran lad works on a piece of metal under the guidance of his teacher, Richard Coger, at Belize Tech.

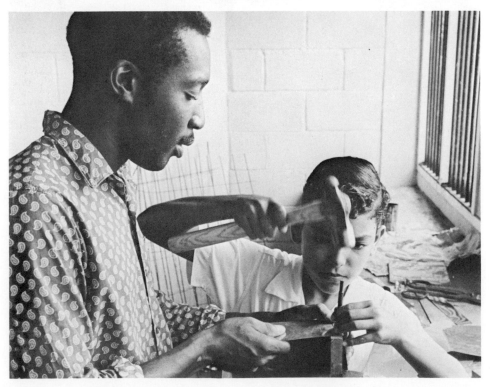

Sometimes they can't even understand each other."

Mrs. Reed, then sixty-nine, was enthusiastic about the Peace Corps and recommended it as a way of life for elderly, retired people. "It is most rewarding," she said. "I want to stress, though, that it is important that they have good health, a tolerant outlook, and a pioneer spirit."

Edwin N. Voirol (Monroeville, Ind.) taught typing and shorthand to the girls in the same school. Then thirty-seven, he had interrupted a teaching career in the Indiana public school system to join the Peace Corps. Drawing on his coaching experience (softball, basketball, and track), he organized a team sports program for the school's 295 girls. Afternoons he coached a men's softball team.

Voirol's roommate, Richard Coger (Pineland, S. C.), also coached softball in the afternoon and toured the back country on weekends playing trumpet with a local band. But his primary assignment was teaching metalworking at Belize Tech. Said Coger, a Negro, of his Peace Corps experience: "It's the best thing that ever happened to me. Every moment is a challenge. It has been a fine thing for my people. They had such crazy notions here about American Negroes. They thought we were a backward, illiterate people."

Andre Colpitts (Tulsa, Okla.) taught chemistry and biology, also at Belize Tech. Colpitts was a graduate student and teaching assistant at the University of Illinois when he joined the Peace Corps. Four nights a week in Belize he taught adult classes, and he got together a science-magic show with which he toured the primary schools in the area.

These are but a few of the Volunteers in that original contingent, and so successful were they all in staffing schools and in training teachers that British Honduras requested thirty-nine more—twenty-six teachers, twelve community development workers, and one road-building supervisor. With continued efforts, British Honduras will have created a self-generating system of education. She will have taken strides to prepare herself for complete independence, and the Peace Corps will have worked itself out of a job.

In the laboratory at Belize Tech, Andre Colpitts explains the properties of a chemical to one of his students.

Colombia

Road building, surveying, digging wells, bridge building, improvement of agriculture, and raising health and sanitation conditions are part of the Peace Corps' rural community action program in Colombia. Working closely with trained Colombian counterparts, the Volunteers' primary objective is selling the self-help idea.

The program is one of several developed by the Peace Corps in cooperation with CARE, an organization already known throughout the world for its self-help activities. Individual projects are administered by CARE, which provides close support and technical guidance under the overall direction and authority of the Peace Corps.

Top, with George Kroon, bareheaded, center, helping, the villagers of Fúquene build a road to bring them and their neighboring communities closer to their markets. Kroon is from Wallingford, Pennsylvania.

On the way to the road-building job, Kroon is accompanied by two of his young admirers.

Asia

As his two years of Peace Corps service approached its end, Volunteer Jim Fisher (Ashland, Ky.) received an invitation. Why not join him, Sir Edmund Hillary asked, in an expedition through the lower Himalayas? The original conquerer of Mt. Everest explained that he was planning more than a mere climb. Working for the government of Nepal, Hillary hoped to bring community development to a number of isolated, almost inaccessible Nepalese villages.

For Fisher, the invitation opened the door to a great adventure. As far as the Peace Corps was concerned, he would be doing valuable work. Fisher asked that his term of service be extended six months, and the Peace Corps agreed that he could join Hillary's expedition of community development workers as a Peace Corps Volunteer. It was a big change from his previous job as a university teacher in mountain-flanked Nepal. Community development took him into what some travelers have described as the most spectacular landscape on earth, right to the base of immense Everest itself.

Few Peace Corps jobs are so touched by romance, though some Volunteers have insisted that "it all depends on how you look at it, and there are times when even the dullest job seems adventurous and exciting." For most of them, the glamour of far-away places is quickly eroded in the day-to-day round of plain hard work that lies at the heart of Peace Corps service. Jim Fisher found it that way, too, when he was still teaching, despite all the wonder of Nepal, where even his latrine "commanded the vast panorama from Annapurna to Everest."

"As the days have merged into weeks," Fisher wrote home, "and the weeks have been absorbed by fleeting months, a measure of understanding, sometimes tacit and always tentative, reveals why these people are as they are. Frustration begins to lose itself in understanding, defeats fade into small accomplishments, and I discover I am learning more than I am teaching."

Peace Corps teaching programs were requested by many nations of Asia and the Far East. Volunteers started to teach in Nepal in October, 1962, one year after the first Far East Volunteers arrived to teach in the Philippines. More than seven hundred Volunteers were soon at work in the Philippines, this program becoming the largest Peace Corps effort in one nation and remaining so until the Colombia program surpassed it in late 1964. Volunteer teachers were assigned to the Philippines' most remote *barrios*, where they found themselves summoned to join in the life of the community. "A *barrio* school is a community school; a Volunteer soon finds that he belongs to the community as much as to the school," Sara Gay Beacham wrote from Basilan Island, one of the Philippines' southernmost islands.

Volunteer Beacham (La Jolla, Calif.) soon found herself adjusting to the life of the community rather than the other way around. "Blinded by initial enthusiasm, I jumped at every chance to teach or to meet new people, to be met with tolerant or quizzical smiles—sometimes laughter."

After a time, she found that she was laughing also "at *merienda* (afternoon tea), with the other teachers, about the way I bumbled my first attempts at bargaining in the dialect, or over how I wanted to work through siesta." Still later: "While we were planning future lessons, one of the teachers said to me, 'How your English has improved since you first came to this place!' We found ourselves laughing together."

Still other education programs were mounted in Indonesia, Malaysia, Thailand, India, Pakistan, Afghanistan, Iran, Turkey and Cyprus. As in Africa, most Volunteer teachers in Asia found themselves assigned to secondary schools—although teaching programs never came to dominate Peace Corps activity in Asia as they did in Africa. Asia, in its incredible variety, summoned the Peace Corps to a variety of activities.

Agriculture programs were organized for India, Pakistan, Nepal, Iran, and Turkey. Urban community development Volunteers went to work in the cities of Turkey and Malaysia. Rural community development workers were assigned to country villages in Turkey and Malaysia, too, and also in India, Pakistan, Nepal, Iran, and the Philippines. Health programs were developed for Thailand, Malaysia, Afghanistan, Pakistan, India, and Turkey. Public works programs were developed for Afghanistan and Pakistan.

To list these categories is barely to hint at the diversity of individual jobs to which Volunteers were assigned. Three Volunteers helped survey the timber resources of Malaya, preparatory to establishing a system of national forests. Another helped survey the fresh-water resources of Sarawak. Bob Burns (St. Louis, Mo.) developed a floodproof irrigation system that saved a valuable Pakistan rice harvest from destruction. Jim Grant (Zionsville, Pa.) helped Iran's tea growers along the Caspian Sea increase their income by planting string beans between the tea bushes. In his spare time, Grant invented a hand-powered washing machine which could be made from an empty oil drum for about fifteen dollars and was much easier on clothing than the rocks in the rivers. Janet Hanneman (Junction City, Kan.) helped modernize a hospital for mental patients in Lahore, Pakistan.

On December 18, 1961, the twenty-four members of India's first Peace Corps program stepped off an airplane in New Delhi. After a few days of orientation, they moved north to the Punjab, where they set about organizing a number of agricultural projects. On the face of it, two dozen Volunteers would seem to have little chance to affect a society which numbers 441,000,000 people. The flat, semiarid state of Punjab alone contains 20,000,000.

Undismayed by statistics, six Volunteers of this small Peace Corps group decided that chickens and eggs offered the quickest way of increasing the protein content of the local diet. The first of what came to be known as the Peace Corps' "Punjab Poultry Pundits" were Sean Doherty (Schaumberg, Ill.), Ken Sherper (Minneapolis, Minn.), Tom Kessinger (Ridgewood, N. J.), Bill Donovan (South Weymouth, Mass.), Justin McLaughlin (Savquoit, N.Y.), and Frank Ziegler (Bellingham, Wash.).

Step One, the Pundits decided, was to put an end to letting chickens run loose. But penned chickens have to be fenced, housed, and fed—all matters involving expense. The Volunteers developed fencing methods that required almost no expense beyond the labor necessary for installation. They experimented and came up with a chicken house costing fifty dollars that was capable of sheltering one hundred layers (at last report Volunteers were still working to bring the price down). They found that the rice hulls which piled up as waste products of the rice milling process could be used as a combination of feed and litter. They published pamphlets in Punjabi and English on how to raise chickens. The price of the pamphlets was one penny. Although they got the pamphlets into circulation, no one was putting their ideas into action.

The six decided that they would have to show Indian villagers that penned chickens could be raised at a profit. They convinced several youth groups to try out their system as a fund-raising device. It worked. And as the youth groups suddenly found they had some money in the bank, the ordinary Punjabi farmers began to take notice. The Volunteer poultry pamphlet had explained (in the English version, directed at fellow Volunteers): "The obstacles are insurmountable. If you figure you can solve these problems, you are nuts." But soon, enough Punjabi farmers were raising chickens and eggs according to the Volunteers' system to form them into producer cooperatives. As members of cooperatives, individual farmers found they could raise a little money on credit. They found it much easier to get financing from India's Five-Year Plan for agricultural development.

The six Poultry Pundits completed their term of Peace Corps service in the summer of 1963. They were replaced. In May of 1965, their replacements were replaced and the Punjab poultry project went rolling on. By 1965 hundreds of farmers in the Pun-

jab were getting thousands of eggs daily from disease-free chickens raised in penned chicken yards. An Indian official said of the Volunteers involved, "They are really catalysts. We already knew about the things they are doing. We have done them, too, on a small scale. But they provided the force and energy necessary to catalyze the villagers into action."

In its fourth year, the poultry project ran into new problems, and these called for new ingenuity on the part of the new Poultry Pundits. The supply of rice hulls ran out, and a new source of inexpensive feed had to be found. So many eggs were then being produced that marketing had now become a major problem. At least half the eggs were getting smashed between the henhouses and the store counters. But as one of the new Pundits said, "They used to smash the Coke bottles, too, and someone solved the transportation problems, and now you can get a Coke anywhere in India. We'll figure out some way to transport eggs."

This is the attitude—and this is the kind of project—that brought the government of the Philippines to honor the Volunteers of Asia and the Far East with the Magsaysay Award, the "Nobel Prize of Asia."

The Punjab Poultry Pundits are among those Volunteers in Asia who elicited a remarkable statement from Thanat Khoman, Foreign Minister of Thailand. At ceremonies in Bangkok's Chulalongkorn University, in which Sargent Shriver was awarded an honorary degree, Thanat said:

"We have always known that America was strong, militarily speaking—that it was a very wealthy nation and that it was one of the two or three most powerful nations in the world today. But we have not known in Thailand the secret of America's power and strength. Today through the Peace Corps, we have come to realize that the strength of America rests in its ideas and ideals. The Peace Corps represents the ideals of America and is the most powerful new force in the world today."

Cyprus

Lying in the eastern end of the Mediterranean Sea just forty miles off the coast of Turkey, the island nation of Cyprus re-enacts in the 1960's scenes from a drama —the oscillating contest between Europe and Asia—that has been played and replayed on her soil since before Homer. East and West, represented by Turks and Greeks, meet today in Cyprus. But they do not merge.

Cyprus is the only country the Peace Corps has had to abandon because of war. The first Volunteers, a contingent of twenty-three, arrived in September, 1962; the last Volunteer departed on March 19, 1964. Hostilities between Greek and Turkish Cypriots reached such proportions that the Volunteers were inhibited in their movements and were prevented from carrying out assignments. Violence was never directed against them by either side.

Cypriot society is cut in two from top to bottom along an ethnic line: governmental representation, municipal administrations, schools, coffee shops, living areas are all designated and separated on that basis. Greek farmers paint their carts blue and the Turks paint theirs red. To add to the host of difficulties that Peace Corps Volunteers expect to encounter wherever they serve, in Cyprus they were handicapped by having to avoid any show of partisanship; if they were in a mixed community and went to a Greek coffee shop one night, they had to go to a Turkish one the next.

Geologists Robert L. Major (Pittsburgh, Pa.) and Alva E. (Gene) Saucier (Alexandria, La.) lived in the village of Komi Kebir on the Karpas Peninsula, a bony finger about fifty miles long, pointing to the northeast. The village had a population of 900, all but 40 of whom were Greek. The Volunteers conducted a geological survey of 125 square miles of land on the peninsula; other geologists in other regions performed similar surveys, which were needed to make effective use of water supplies and mineral deposits.

High above the coastal plain of Cyprus' Karpas Peninsula, geologists Gene Saucier and Robert Major take rock samples. Saucier, far left, and Major, left, examine samples through magnifying glasses before sending them to Nicosia for analysis.

The people of Komi Kebir could not understand why the Americans had come to their village. Rumors spread that they were either working for an American oil company or looking for a Polaris submarine site. (The left-wing press in Cyprus tried to discredit the Peace Corps from the start by calling the Volunteers spies, *agents provocateurs*, and incompetents.) Using their work maps and rock samples, Major and Saucier took great pains to explain exactly what they were doing.

"The first question we were always asked was how much money we were making," Gene Saucier said. "Even the shepherds wanted to know right away when we met them. And there was always

A coffehouse in Komi Kebir. Robert Major passes an evening over a backgammon board with a villager.

With an admiring audience looking on, Dominic V. Marino (New York City) takes his turn at the end of a jump rope. Marino was the athletic coach for one girls' school and five boys' schools in Nicosia.

a look of disbelief on their faces when we told them."

The pair rented a room from a spry Greek farmer and took their meals with his family. They hauled their water in jugs from a spigot two blocks away. Their only diversion was in the town's coffee shop where, after the villagers had accepted them as everybody's friends, they were expected to show up regularly. Once every two weeks they drove their Land Rover to Nicosia for a hot bath.

Buoyed up by British and American aid, Cyprus is a near-prosperous country, second only to Israel in that part of the world for economic development. What it needs, assuming that internal antagonisms can be resolved, is to make itself independent of foreign assistance. That's where the Peace Corps came in. Besides geologists (Cyprus had only one qualified geologist of its own when the Peace Corps was there), the country lacks teachers and technicians of many kinds; on other parts of the island Volunteers were connected with schools, farms, and industries.

The four-fifths majority of Greeks says it wants union with Greece; the Turkish minority says it wants partition of the island. Both sides are caching heavy stores of arms. As long as this tense situation prevails the Peace Corps will not return to Cyprus. But diplomatic agreements provide that with the establishment of a reliable peace Volunteers will once again work among the Cypriots.

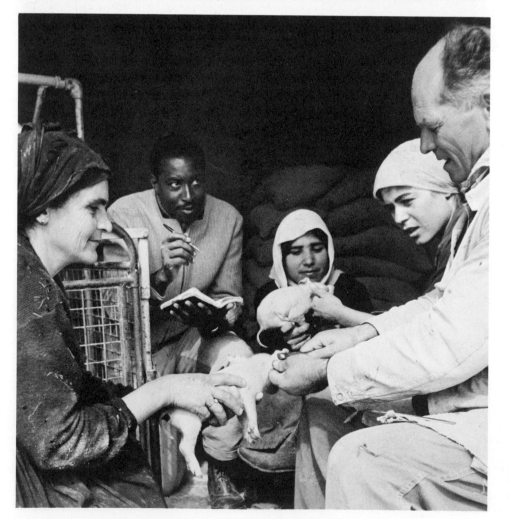

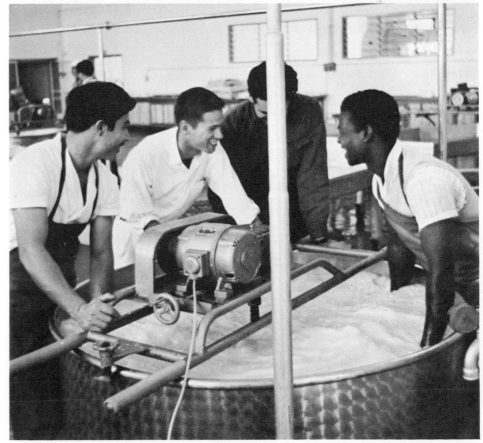

Turkey

The territory over which modern Turkey extends has been the scene of endless migrations and changes of rule going back over thousands of years. Archeological diggings have brought up remains of the Hittites, Medes, Persians, Trojans, Greeks, Romans, Moguls, and Armenians—an abbreviated list.

In the eleventh century A.D. the Turks themselves invaded from the Middle East, taking all of Asia Minor from the Byzantine Empire. These were the Seljuk Turks,

Top, the new Middle East Technical University on the outskirts of Ankara. To the west, at the left, the ground has been planted with a million pine trees—the John F. Kennedy Memorial Grove. The English preparatory school, a small cluster of buildings, is right of center and just beyond the main campus.

A farmer and his team on the Anatolian plateau.

A mechanic watches as Alfred Carpeno demonstrates a hydraulic press built in his equipment repair shop in the city of Mersin.

A farmer and his family gather around Carpeno for a friendly chat in a field that adjoins the shop.

who defended their territory and Moslem culture against the Crusaders. Around 1300 they in turn succumbed to the Osmanli Turks, who established the Ottoman Empire and eventually crushed Byzantium. The Empire lasted until the First World War, which brought about its collapse and partition into spheres of privilege by European powers propping up a helpless ruler. Led by Kemal Ataturk, Turkey fought a war of independence from 1920 to 1922; after the abolition of the Caliphate in 1924 it became a republic, and an aspiring people began the great task of building a modern nation, a task which is still to be completed.

More than a thousand miles long and four hundred miles wide, the country has a variety of scenery and climates. Along the Black Sea runs the Pontic chain of mountains, ranging from two to eleven thousand feet. Along the Mediterranean Sea stretch the Taurus Mountains. The great, fertile Anatolian plateau lies between these two mountain ranges.

Economic and social conditions vary as

Left, Alfred Carpeno gives Turkish mechanics pointers on repairing part of a bulldozer in the Mersin repair shop.

Bottom left, English teacher Larry Fisher (Seattle, Wash.) thumbs through an American magazine with three of his students in Gaziantep, on the Syrian border.

Bottom right, a patriarch of the town of Ceyhan.

much as the topography and climate. In the cities exists the modern world of schools, industry, and electricity. In the villages time stands still. People live as their ancestors did. Medical help, education, sanitation, and sophisticated agricultural methods are sorely lacking.

Ataturk's revolution, however, is still going on; many new schools are being built, and the study of English is stressed. As a result, there is a growing need for teachers of English, a need which the Peace Corps is trying to help fill.

Turkey's outstanding achievement in the field of education is the Middle East Technical University on the outskirts of Ankara, which, when completed, will undoubtedly be the finest institution of its kind in the Near East. Some forty-five

Right, a street scene in Cankiri.

An off-duty visit is paid to a coffeehouse in Ceyhan by Steve Allen, in white shirt, right, playing backgammon, and Carl Olson, wearing glasses, center left, chatting with Turkish friends. Both are teachers. Steve is from San Francisco, and Carl comes from Hockessin, Delaware.

hundred students are already attending classes in the twelve buildings that have been erected. Eighteen more buildings will be added, and the enrollment is expected to reach fifteen thousand. Five Peace Corps Volunteers are on the regular faculty, and there are nineteen more in the adjoining English preparatory school.

Typical of Volunteers who have taught in Turkey are a young couple named Allan and Margaret Ann Gall (Lesterville, S. D.). They were English teachers in Cankiri, a military center northeast of Ankara. Their school was badly understaffed, with only fifteen teachers for fifteen hundred pupils.

"I found the children adorable," Peggy said. "I loved them individually, but eighty eleven- and twelve-year-olds at once were too many."

The Galls rented a small four-room apartment with indoor plumbing for fifteen dollars a month. Coal was rationed to one ton for the winter season, but they managed to save some for chilly spring nights. Good fruit and vegetables were plentiful in Cankiri but the meat supply was limited. Hamburger and shish kebob were treats.

The Galls led a full social life. When

Peggy Gall walks home from school through Cankiri with some of her students.

Below left, Peggy teaching English grammar.

Two of Peggy's students.

There is no dearth of vegetables in this market in Cankiri where Peggy has come to shop after school.

Right, she buys some yogurt at a local store.

Bottom, supper over, Peggy washes the dishes in her small kitchen.

they arrived, scores of persons called to welcome them. In fact, socializing later threatened to interfere with their work. So many people, seeing lights burning in their apartment, would pay evening visits that precious time for grading papers was lost. They couldn't offend their Turkish friends by refusing visitors, yet the papers had to be graded. The Galls resolved this dilemma by grading papers by flashlight.

Numerous, too, in the contingents that are being sent to Turkey are home economists, who are expanding the knowledge of child care, home management, nutrition, and food preparation, and community development workers, who are creating self-help programs in the villages and on the farms.

One of the Volunteers working in community development was Alfred Carpeno (Providence, R. I.), whose primary job was in a heavy-equipment repair shop in Mersin, a port on the Mediterranean. He was unusually versatile. Not only did he advise his Turkish co-workers in the care

In January, 1964, Director Sargent Shriver made a trip around the world, stopping in a number of countries to inspect Peace Corps operations. Here he visits an orphanage in the city of Konya, where three Volunteers were stationed. With Janet Bullock (Vallejo, Calif.) looking on, one of the orphans gets his special attention.

Nurse Susan Cleveland (Canton, Mass.) shows a student nurse how to read a thermometer in Konya.

and handling of heavy equipment, but he also helped to construct machines such as a hydraulic press, which was mostly made out of scrap parts. At night he taught English to the shop's mechanics, and with knowledge gained from an extension course in horticulture at Harvard, he advised neighboring farmers how to improve their vegetable crops.

Returning Volunteers are enthusiastic about the warm reception they received from the Turks. A Turkish provincial education officer said:

"Rightly or wrongly, we think of ourselves as a people with a past filled with accomplishments, but temporarily left far

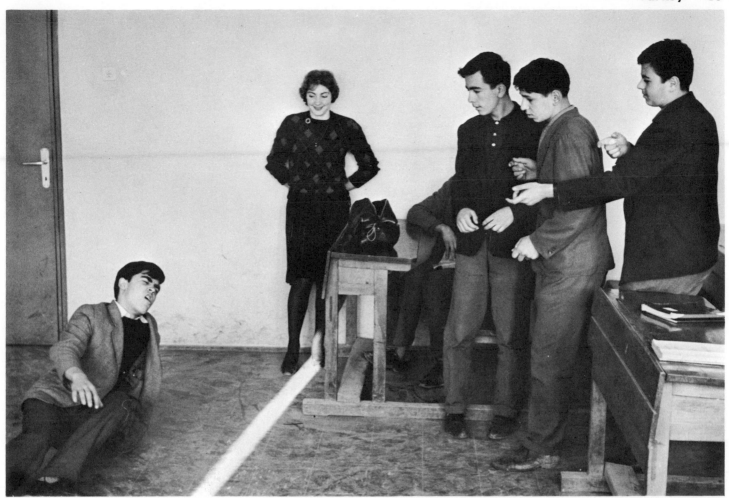

Jean Zettlemoyer (Lehighton, Pa.), an imaginative English teacher, center, had her students in Bursa write skits, which they then acted out in class. In one of these plays, three "hunters" stalk and shoot a "tiger," writhing on the floor.

Agriculture extension agents Robert Nunn, center, and David Kunkel, behind him, wearing glasses, watch as two farmers doctor a horse's mouth in the village of Runkush, on the Anatolian plateau south of Ankara. Kunkel (Pocatello, Ida.) and Nunn (Edinburg, Tex.) worked among the farmers getting them to cull poor animals from the flocks and to rotate their pasture land. The Volunteers had ten villages on their circuit.

behind by many other nations. In our eagerness to catch up, we have to accept material aid—sometimes even food to eat. Our gratitude for such aid is diluted with a measure of shame that we have fallen into such a state that we must accept gifts and loans.

"What the Peace Corps is doing is something infinitely more appreciated. It is aid that is acceptable without any sense of unfulfillable obligation. These people are giving something they can give: they are giving themselves."

Afghanistan

Americans have long cherished cities of the East in exotic images: mosques gleaming in the sun; mazes of bazaars teeming with beasts and humans; strange music, noise, fetid odors languishing in the air; dark, turbaned men; robes, sandals; camels, carts, hawkers, charlatans; heat.

Such is Kabul, capital of Afghanistan. Four hundred thousand of the nearly 14,000,000 Afghans dwell there. Surrounding the city are peaks of the Hindu Kush, a chain of mountains fifteen to sixteen thousand feet high.

Afghans branch from ancient Persian stock, in two principal groups—Pashtuns and Tajiks—and two minority groups—

Top, Istalif, a town near Kabul, in the foothills of the Hindu Kush.

Director of the Peace Corps, Sargent Shriver, talks to a camel driver in a caravan he met while driving by jeep from Kabul to Pakistan. It was springtime and the caravan was heading north for the sheep-grazing season.

A busy thoroughfare in the heart of Kabul. The Hindu Kush tower over the capital city.

Frank T. Brechin oversees the work of an Afghan mechanic in the large Kabul garage where he was a foreman.

Uzbeks and Hazaras. Afghanistan grows fruit and raises some four million head of sheep, and its chief export is wool. Pashto is the official language, but the favored tongue is Farsi (Persian); English, the study of which is being promoted by the government, ranks a poor third. Nearly all Afghans follow the Moslem faith.

When the first Peace Corps Volunteers went to Kabul in September, 1962, they were treated, like all foreigners, as guests. And as guests they were subject to all the privileges and restrictions commensurate with that status. The Afghans expected unquestioned acceptance of every hospitality and rigid obedience of their rules of decorum. They were disturbed that the Americans did not act like other tourists.

The English teachers, nurses, and the single mechanic—nine in all—were received with courtesy and a distant reserve. They were shown expensive housing and

Wearing a karakul hat, David Fleishhacker calls for an answer in one of his English classes. The fleece of which the hat is made is a principal Afghan export.

While an Afghan student nurse assists, Dorothy Luketich (Armonk, N. Y.) cleans a baby's infected eyes in a Kabul hospital.

risked offending their hosts by not accepting. It took a while and the arrival of more Volunteers, but the Afghans eventually perceived that their "guests" had not come to vacation but to work, that they hadn't much money to spend on housing, and that they were prepared to live "like the people." Before long, formality gave way to candid friendships.

The number of Volunteers in Kabul has multiplied since that time (and indeed the Peace Corps, initially restricted to the capital, now works in all parts of the country), but David Fleishhacker (San Francisco, Calif.), an English teacher, and Frank T. Brechin (Grand Rapids, Mich.), an auto mechanic, were among the pioneering nine and took quarters together over a fruit bazaar.

Opposite top, three horsemen ride off into the Hindu Kush, one of Asia's great mountain chains. The peaks in this area reach a height of 16,000 feet. It is spring and the trees are in bloom.

Far left, an Afghan baba, or old man. Left, a farmer bears his calf to market. The farmer, who is one day from his destination, Kabul, has already carried the calf for several days.

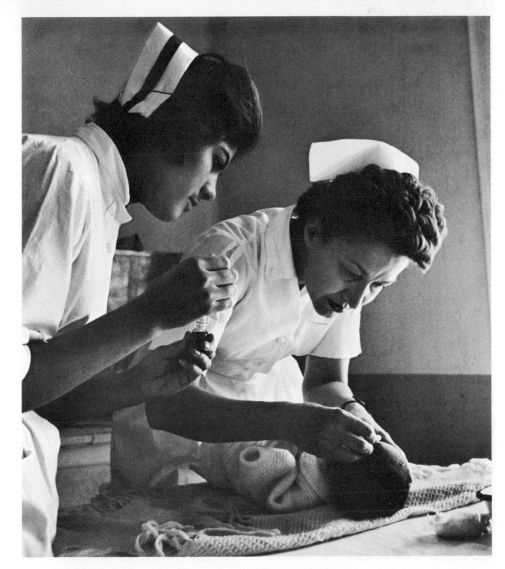

Janet Mueller leads her English Club girls in an American folk song. White scarves are worn by all Afghan schoolgirls.

Left, the Kabul bazaar. Janet Mueller takes a breath and tries to get her bearings in the complex streets. Bottom, she makes a purchase in a stall as Volunteer Jill Rindelaub (Mankato, Minn.) looks on.

Brechin worked in a mammoth, partly government-owned repair shop. He was foreman over ten Afghan mechanics in the service department, which maintained Afghanistan's three hundred Soviet buses and taxis and thirty American buses. The two Russian aides in the shop stayed aloof except when the question of whether Soviet or American techniques were to be used compelled them to consult with the American. By the end of his tour, Brechin had transformed the service department from a deficit operation into the leading money-maker of the garage.

Fleishhacker taught English to two hundred boys in thirty hours of classes per week. Comparing his school in Kabul to the California high school in which he had taught for two years, he said, "There are twice as many students per class and many facilities are lacking. There is little light in the classrooms. During the winter there is no heat. . . . It's not so bad for teachers because we can walk around, but the kids can get awfully cold."

Overcrowded classrooms made discipline difficult, and Moslem traditions of rote learning from the Koran made

students reluctant to venture beyond the strictures of textbooks.

"You meet frustrations at home, too," Fleishhacker said, "but of a different kind. Here you're bucking two thousand years with every step forward. You are constantly pushing against a load of centuries."

Janet Mueller (Kearney, Neb.) was also among the first group in Kabul. She taught English at a girls' school. An accomplished musician, she applied her talents by using American folk songs to teach English. Afghans, teachers for the most part, were entertained frequently in the apartment she shared with two other girls. The Afghans were impressed by the girls' willingness to do without luxuries.

Wandering in the labyrinthine bazaars, in which everything but whiskey and pork could be purchased if one had the fortitude and the time to explore, was a fascinating pastime. Some of the bargains that were found: custom-made leather shoes for as little as three dollars, leather-embroidered coats lined with Persian lamb's wool for twenty dollars, and lapis lazuli jewelry. Bus transportation was cheap at two cents a fare, but the girls had to adjust to segregation of the sexes—females were consigned to the back of the bus.

A showcase of jewelry catches Janet's eye. Right, curious onlookers watch as Janet makes a purchase. Bottom, on the front porch of their apartment Janet, right, and her roommates, Dorothy Luketich, center, and Jill Rindelaub, laugh with their teacher during a Farsi (Persian) lesson.

Pakistan

When Janet Hanneman, who was born on a Kansas farm, went to Pakistan as a Peace Corps Volunteer, she asked to be assigned to the Government Mental Hospital in Lahore. The request was granted, but eyes were raised and people wondered. It was known as "that terrible place."

Janet joined the Peace Corps in August, 1961. She had obtained her B.A. and R.N. from the University of Kansas in 1958, had had six months' experience as a psychiatric nurse at the Maudsley Hospital in London, and on a fellowship had worked toward an M.A. in psychology at Victoria University in Wellington, New Zealand. She arrived in Lahore, West Pakistan, in December, 1961.

Situated on seventy-five acres of land and accommodating one thousand male and five hundred female patients, Lahore's Government Mental Hospital is the largest medical institution of any kind in Pakistan.

When Janet Hanneman reached the hospital, some parts of it resembled a medieval chamber of horrors. Only three hundred of the patients had beds; most of them slept on mats or piles of straw laid over a concrete floor. A few patients had private rooms or dormitory accommodations, but many slept in cells with iron-bar doors, which were kept locked. Many patients had no eating utensiles and had their meals poured into their hands, or even slopped on the floor outside the cell door. Psychotherapy was absent. The hospital was little better than a jail for society's mental untouchables.

The medical superintendent, English-trained Dr. Mohammed Rashid Chaudhry, and a new administrative officer, Dr. Khalid Mahmud Awan, were both capable men who wanted to reform the hospital, and they welcomed Janet's offer to help them. But one scarcely knew where to begin. "At first," said Janet, "I thought I should concentrate on psychotherapeutic care for the patients, but then I decided that their physical comfort

Some of the patients at the Lahore Government Mental Hospital slept on piles of straw . . . and ate like this.

should be improved first. How could you talk to a man about his mental problems when you knew he wasn't getting the proper food?"

So, beginning at the beginning, with the wholehearted cooperation of the two doctors, Janet went to work. She saw that the quality of the patients' food was improved and that every patient was issued a tin plate and bowl. The piles of straw were replaced with beds and mattresses and sheets, obtained at no increase in the hospital's budget. Light blues, yellows, pinks, and greens were painted over stark walls, calendar pictures were hung, curtains were added to windows, and floor mats were provided. Patients' uniforms were changed and sanitation standards raised.

After a year, the padlocks that had secured cells and compounds were discarded. Light and air were brought in and the patients were brought out, and the miraculous transformation was under way.

While it might have been possible for Janet—by cajoling and pestering local, national, and international organizations, government officials, and civic groups for support—to bring about changes in physical conditions, it was patently impossible for her to administer psychotherapeutic care to fifteen hundred patients. Some kind of trained staff had to be recruited. And this was a problem.

Attitudes in Pakistan, as in most of Asia, toward mental illness are still old-fashioned. In fact, the concept of mental *illness* has yet to be formed. Consequently, countries that desperately need doctors and nurses in the first place (in 1962 East Pakistan with a population of 52,000,000 had 100 nurses, and West Pakistan had 1,500 nurses for its 48,000,000 people) suffer from an almost total lack of personnel trained to cope with the mentally ill.

Janet Hanneman supervises an evening meal outside one of the hospital dormitories.

Hospital beds get an airing in a courtyard. Janet reaches out a reassuring hand to a shy, withdrawn patient.

Far left, Janet walks arm in arm with a patient; many of the patients became very fond of her. Left, she discovers an elderly patient who had somehow hurt his head and was lying on the grass. Janet questioned him and then had one of the hospital attendants take care of him. Opposite bottom, Janet inspects the women's section of the hospital.

Open doors behind Janet symbolize her work. Before she came many were locked. Here she listens to a retiring patient who had spoken to no one for months.

The nursing profession itself is considered somewhat degrading. Lahore's Government Mental Hospital, an outstanding example of the results of these obstructive attitudes, served as a dumping ground for incompetent doctors and nurses. Medical personnel were often sent there as a kind of punishment. That Janet Hanneman—a young, attractive American girl—*asked* to be sent there was incredible.

How could one young person reform the attitudes of an entire country? Or even the officialdom? Janet obviously could not. Her attempt, however, was valiant and inspiring, and with her furious activity and complex involvements she started the process of conversion.

She got two Lahore hospitals to send their student nurses for tours of the mental hospital as part of their regular training. Janet helped to found the Lahore Mental Health Association, the first active group of its kind in Pakistan, whose objective is to teach the public about mental illness. Because the Government Mental Hospital offered no outpatient care, Janet instituted a program through which volunteers could help with patient rehabilitation. She was honorary director of nursing for the Lahore district T.B. Association. She lectured on public health nursing at the Institute of Hygiene and Preventive Medicine to doctors working for diplomas. She wrote articles for the *Social Work Review* of Punjab University. She participated in panels and conferences and spoke to women's and youth groups. But, above all, it was the example of her very presence that had the profoundest effect. As one official told her, "By your efforts nursing has almost become a respectable profession in Pakistan."

Janet Hanneman adapted herself thoroughly to the Pakistani way of life. She lived with a local family, spoke their language, and wore Pakistani clothing exclusively. At the end of her tour she

requested a one-year extension. She said at the time, "I want to stay because with an additional year I can do much more than I was able to accomplish during my first two years." Her request was granted. The Peace Corps, which at that time rarely and only for special reasons allowed such extensions, acknowledged a meritorious performance.

Janet Hanneman is only one of about two hundred Volunteers who have served or are serving in Pakistan. The majority of them are participating in public works projects and rural community action programs. Others are agriculture demonstration agents, nurses, or teachers in secondary schools and universities. All are there, of course, by invitation of the Pakistani government, which is trying to alleviate a multitude of afflictions.

Pakistan was created in 1947 as a homeland for the Moslems of British India. East and West Pakistan, one nation, are separated by nearly a thousand miles of India. With 100,000,000 people it is the largest Islamic country in the world, and,

Marching along with their instructor, Willie Douglas (Tampa, Fla.), high school students who belong to a vocational agriculture program head for their classroom—the fields. The scene is Katlang, a remote mountain village in West Pakistan, near the Afghan border.

Below left, Willie Douglas watches as some of his students cultivate their training plots with traditional farm implements.

A Pakistani farmer.

indeed, rampant population growth is its overriding difficulty. Per capita income is about the lowest in Asia and life expectancy is thirty-five years. Only by a Promethean marshaling of its resources, which it does not lack, can Pakistan expect to gain control over population growth, poverty, and disease.

As in poor nations elsewhere, a modern system of agriculture is the indispensable prerequisite to economic development. Pakistan has vast areas of land that can be put to the plow, but her already large irrigation system must be expanded to water the arid regions; flood control systems must be constructed to harness the monsoon, which brings sixty inches of rain to West Pakistan, floods the land,

Wheat in the school's field is ready for harvesting. Willie Douglas explains the techniques of examining the ripe grain to test its quality.

Harvesting grain in the extreme northwestern corner of West Pakistan near the Afghan border. A two-wheeled cart holds the harvest. At left, behind the cart, one of the farmer's oxen rests.

Pakistani electrical engineering students gather around their instructor, Marian D. Owen (Seattle, Wash.), as she works out a problem on the blackboard at the West Pakistan University of Engineering and Technology.

Jack B. Duff (Adams, Ore.) and a Pakistani mechanic fix a broken tractor at a cooperative farming project in a West Pakistan village. The 120 villages in the project bought 65 tractors and are using them cooperatively. Duff and another Volunteer organized repair and maintenance facilities.

washes away topsoil, and leaves the country dry for the rest of the year; new crops, hybrid seed, contour plowing, fertilization, crop rotation—all the advances of modern agriculture—must be taught to the farmers; highways must be built to carry harvests from the hinterlands to the crowded cities.

Inconspicuously, perhaps, in this densely populated land, the Peace Corps Volunteers contribute a seasoning of good will, enthusiasm, and know-how. They reach the very roots of society, most of them offering nothing more than a willingness to help and the skills they grew up with. In a brochure sent to prospective Pakistan-bound Volunteers, one finds the following remarkable statement: "You will probably have acquired many of the basic skills you will need in Pakistan just by having lived twenty-odd years or more. Being able to build and repair things, being able to get along with all kinds of people, to teach them and to like them is what you need and you will bring these things with you."

Nepal

Barbara Wylie can look back on it now and laugh, but at the time she was frightened.

"One night two men started following me as I was walking home to our house in Katmandu. They followed me down one dark alley after another, and finally caught up with me just as I reached our gate. I was scared to death."

This Peace Corps Volunteer from Ann Arbor, Michigan, need not have worried. All they wanted, the men blurted out, was for her to teach them English. Vastly relieved, she told them to come back the next afternoon for their first lesson.

A few days later, at the post office, she was approached by a clerk who asked if he

Top, Nepalese bearers stop for a rest on the narrow stone-covered main street of Pokhara, a town of about 10,000 people ninety miles west of Katmandu, Nepal's capital. Behind Pokhara the massive Annapurna range of the Himalayas rises.

Barbara Wylie, a Volunteer English teacher, rides through an outlying village, in which one of her schools was located, on her way back to Katmandu.

could become a student, too. Soon a half-dozen adults dropped around for Barbara's afternoon classes, which she held in the rambling old house in Katmandu that she and two other Volunteers rented from a former Nepalese politician.

Lying between India and Tibet, Nepal, with an area of 54,000 square miles, has a population of more than 9,000,000, making its population density three times that of the United States. Until a revolution in 1950, Nepal was almost totally inaccessible to the outside world. It is a land of great geographical extremes, with dense jungle in the south and the gigantic Himalayas in the north. Located on the Tibetan frontier one hundred miles northeast of Katmandu, Nepal's capital, is Mt. Everest, which was reconquered in 1963 by an expedition of American climbers. One of the five Americans to reach the top was William F. Unsoeld (Corvallis, Ore.), the Peace Corps' Nepal Representative. (Representatives in the Peace Corps, popularly called "Reps," supervise operations within an entire country.)

English instruction in Nepal, which has

Barbara Wylie teaches a group of "Untouchable" children in Katmandu. Below, a WHO medical technician inoculates a pupil against smallpox as Barbara watches.

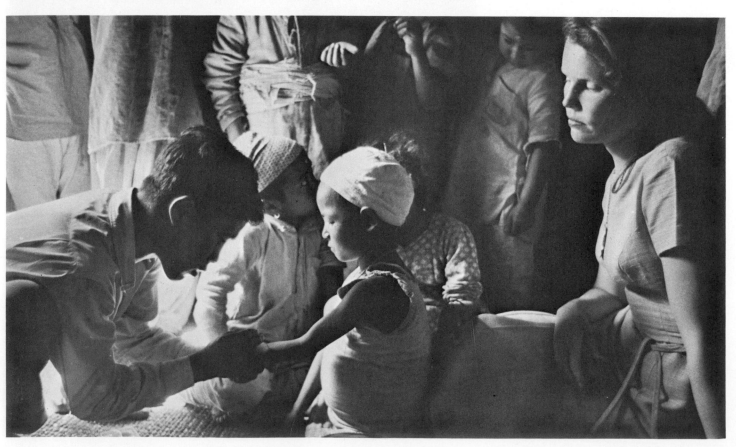

Barbara and two friends ride along the sacred Baghmati River in Katmandu. Right, in a near-by village, Barbara is surrounded by her pupils.

one of the world's lowest literacy rates (between 2 and 9 per cent), has taken on an air of urgency. Thousands of persons must be trained to use the language that has been adopted for commerce and higher education. The Peace Corps is helping by supplying qualified teachers.

Barbara Wylie, a Volunteer teacher, arrived in Katmandu in September, 1962. One day she discovered from a friend that the children of the low-caste servants—the cooks, gatekeepers, gardeners—in the neighborhood were getting no schooling at all.

"I hit upon the idea of teaching them. I took a few slates and some chalk over to my friend's house one morning and we began. To start with there were five children, but everything soon snowballed. Now we have fifty students coming each morning, sitting around our little red, blue, and green tables, and filling the courtyard fuller and fuller. But since nobody has to come, everyone seems happy about the situation—so much so that the students have named it Happy Free School."

Along with English lessons, Barbara gave rudimentary health instruction to the women of a village outside Katmandu. "I explained to them in my bad Nepali things such as typhoid coming from bad water. I tell them they should boil it, especially in the monsoon season. I tell

A farmer plows in the shadow of the Nepalese center of Lamaist Buddhism in Boddhnath, a village three miles from Katmandu. On every side of the temple in the background are painted a huge pair of eyes, the all-seeing eyes of God.

A wandering Nepalese musician plays his three-stringed instrument.

them they should build their latrines away from their houses, and not go to the bathroom in the street. I try to explain to them that they can raise their gardens without using human manure."

Barbara shared her three rooms with two Peace Corps workers, two Indian families, a Nepalese family, and a Tibetan family. She gave English lessons to the women.

One of the Volunteers who shared the house with Barbara Wylie was Lulu A. Miller, a retired schoolteacher from Arlington, Virginia. In her sixties, Miss Miller was the oldest Volunteer in the project. Her youthful outlook on life was

Leslie Gile shows a farm girl the chicks he has brought her family. Gile bought two thousand chicks from a local hatchery and distributed them to the farmers in the Pokhara area, keeping thirty for himself. Because good feed is expensive, the typical Nepalese farmer lets his chickens fend for themselves. After six weeks Gile's chicks, which had been fed a balanced diet, were so much larger than the farmers' that they became very interested in his methods.

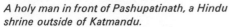

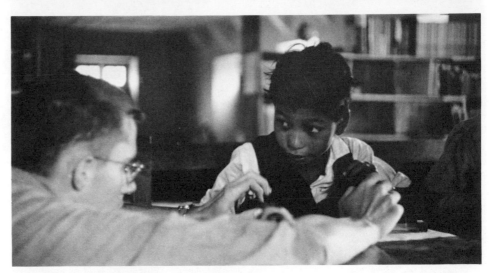

A holy man in front of Pashupatinath, a Hindu shrine outside of Katmandu.

Top right, a youngster studies the tool Bertold Puchtler (Vestal, N. Y.) is using in his carpentry class in Pokhara.

Right, George P. Peck (Colorado Springs, Colo.) explains a science problem in the Balaju school for boys in Katmandu.

Bottom right, Glenda Warren (Fort Bliss, Tex.) teaches girls to sew at Meen Bhawan, a training school on the edge of Katmandu. Glenda's students later taught rural women simple homemaking skills.

Below, Nepal has many Tibetan refugees, like this mother and child who, having fled Tibet when the Chinese Communists took over, live on the outskirts of Katmandu.

Lulu Miller and two of her biology students look over a jar of pond algae that she had collected on the grounds of Tri Chandra College in Katmandu.

Miss Miller and her students discuss the mechanics of flight as they dissect a pigeon wing at Tri Chandra.

best shown on the first day of school when she arrived riding sidesaddle on a motor scooter driven by a Nepalese student. She taught biology six days a week at Tri Chandra College and, like many of the Volunteers in Nepal, gave English lessons to her students on the side.

An innovation that she introduced at the school was frequent testing. Students were being tested only once every two years, but Miss Miller persuaded her department head that it would be to the students' advantage to take them on a twice-a-month basis.

The Nepalese diet tended to be monotonous, with too much rice and not enough meat, but Miss Miller was an imaginative cook. One day she served Nepalese members of the science department a drink that she had concocted from a local berry. Her guests had never tasted the drink before and were astonished that it came from something they had been familiar with all their lives.

There was no doubt in Miss Miller's mind that her upbringing in rural Virginia had prepared her for any discomforts she encountered in Katmandu. "We knew what it was for a cistern to go dry, and, of course, there was no electricity on the farm. During the winter it used to get cold at home and we had to bundle up, too."

The experiences of Leslie Gile (Rochester, N. H.) were quite different. He and Mark C. Shroeder (Belvidere, Vt.) worked on a twelve-acre experimental farm run by the government a mile outside Pokhara, a town of 10,000 people located ninety miles west of Katmandu. Under the supervision of the Volunteers and a Nepalese farm manager, trial patches of wheat, corn, rice, and peanuts were planted with varying amounts of fertilizer and with different seed concentrations to see what would produce the best yield.

The importance of this sort of work is great in a country like Nepal, with its predominantly agricultural economy. About 90 per cent of the people depend on the soil for their livelihood. There is enough arable land in Nepal to support her population, but because of primitive farming practices, food production is low and the threat of famine hangs over many areas.

A person with an inventive turn of mind, Gile devised a new halter and new bullock yoke for the local farmers to try. He also introduced a metal-bladed plow that turns over much more earth than the Nepalese one.

A major undertaking for Gile and Shroeder was helping to build a fence around the farm to keep buffaloes from trampling the crops. Barbed wire is unknown in Pokhara; most fences are laboriously made of stone and resemble those seen in New England. While the fence was being erected, Gile learned a

Top, a mother and child rest alongside a stone wall near Pokhara.

Julie Goetze (Brookline, Mass.) with three physics students at Katmandu's Public Science College. Julie was in Nepal with her husband Rolf, an architect, whose most notable achievement was designing a college at Pokhara.

Left, wearing Nepalese clothing, James Fisher, an English teacher, rides his bicycle through the streets of a village in the Katmandu valley.

Bottom, Jim jokes with his colleagues on the Katmandu College of Education staff.

lesson that other Volunteers have had to learn the world over: it isn't always easy to help others help themselves.

"My theory was to show them how to build the fence, but then let them build it themselves, even though it took a couple of weeks longer. That's the only way they would learn," Gile said.

"While we were fencing I wanted to show them how to make a better corner. They told me I was too young and wouldn't know what was best. They really got angry. You have to watch yourself constantly to see that you are not pushing them too fast. They don't appreciate being pushed and balk. I wasn't sure myself of the corner, and I was lucky that it turned out as well as it did."

Two of the most difficult things with which the Volunteers at Pokhara had to contend were a feeling of isolation and a monotonous, unnourishing diet. In all of Nepal there are only three hundred miles of roads fit for vehicles, and Pokhara can be reached only by air or on foot. During the summer months when the monsoon closes in around the area, the town is inaccessible by air. Should a Volunteer find it necessary to get to Katmandu for any reason, he would have to trek for six days over precarious mountain footpaths.

James F. Fisher (Ashland, Ky.), later to climb the lower Himalayas with Sir Edmund Hillary, lived with a local family in Bhaktapur, a village not far from Katmandu. His landlord, Krishna Raj, was a retired civil servant and a Brahman, which meant that Jim could not eat with the family, but had his two meals a day served to him in his room. Jim usually dressed Nepalese style, in a *mayalposh suwal* and a black *topi* hat.

Fisher taught English at the demonstration school attached to the College of Education in Katmandu and at the Nepal-American Center, which enrolled adults the American government planned to

Opposite top, playing barker at a carnival, Jim holds a chicken to be raffled off later. The carnival was organized by Volunteers to raise money for a destitute boys' school.

Right, Jim holds his English class on the lawn of the College of Education in Katmandu.

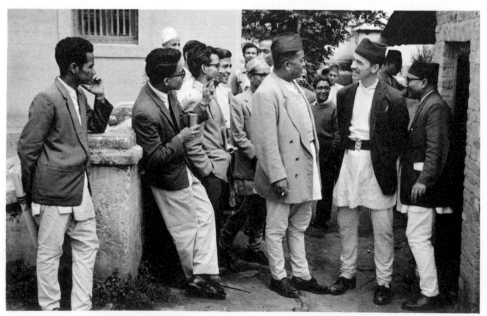

Gary Schaller (Maynard, Minn.) teaches English in a small crowded classroom in Banepat, sixteen miles from Katmandu.

Joyce Thorkelson (Patterson, Calif.) and her students outside the demonstration school of Katmandu's College of Education.

send to the United States. An Eagle Scout, Jim became an adviser and a leader of the newly organized Nepalese scout movement.

During his winter vacation, he traveled around the country taking pictures. His trip included an eight-day trek, without maps, through the southern jungle, one of the best tiger hunting areas in the world. Wrote Fisher:

"I'm extremely happy here. I've found it a challenge, not only in the more romantic sense of the word, but also in the sense of learning to cope with daily frustrations. I find it illuminating in that it brings into perspective a number of the issues which we argue and read about, such as economic development, the advantages that Communism may enjoy, and how we can best combat it."

Thailand

Thailand alone among Southeast Asian countries was never a colony of a Western power; it therefore has little anti-Western feeling in an area of the world that knows much of it. Formerly called Siam, Thailand is about the size of Texas and in 1962 had a population of 28,000,000. There are no large cities other than Bangkok, the capital, where 2,000,000 people live.

Most Thai people make their living from agriculture. Major commodities are rice, tin, teak, and rubber. Except for Moslem influence in the south, most of the population is Buddhist. Few people practice their religion more actively than the Thais. Most men, including the kings, serve some period in the priesthood and every town, no matter how small, has its graceful *wat*, or temple.

The Thai language, whose alphabet is based on Sanskrit, is spoken throughout the country, but the study of English is being stressed more and more. A Thai must know English to attend a university, study abroad, or advance in government and society. Books on mathematics, science, and other technical subjects, even authoritative works on Thai history, are available only in English. Few Thais are qualified to teach this widely accepted second language.

The Peace Corps has been asked to help fill the void of English teachers. Two of the several hundred Volunteers who have served in Thailand are Mark Hawthorne and his wife, Betty, of New York City. While Mark was in Bangkok, he described his experiences.

"Nothing upsets a Volunteer quite so much as praise. It is a blow to those arriving in Thailand to find that they are even more popular here than they were in the U. S. . . .

"Women Volunteers say they are constantly told how beautiful they are, but few complain about this. Similarly, men Volunteers often hear how strong and handsome they are. A Volunteer need only say two words in Thai to be told he speaks it superbly.

"But all this popularity often distresses Volunteers. For one thing, Volunteers realize that popularity isn't enough. A school that struggles to get a Volunteer and displays him prominently at ceremonies may insist that he teach every class

in the school for an hour a week. . . .

"Another problem is a more subtle one. Said one Volunteer, 'I was in my town for six months and thought everything was wonderful. Everyone was so friendly, so polite. About the seventh month I began to realize that I really didn't know anything about the town or the people. I had a feeling that they had been fending me off with praise, keeping me at arm's distance. I haven't entirely lost this feeling yet.'"

The warmth shown to Volunteers is an extension of native Thai friendliness, but it also reflects a satisfaction with the status

A small village in central Thailand. These houses on stilts are typical of the country, being made of hardwoods, often teak.

quo. However, to the Western eye and the eyes of Thailand's leaders, something must be done about the contradiction between gilded temples and the deep poverty in which so many Thais live, between sophistication and culture on the one hand and ignorance, apathy, and disease on the other.

One of Thailand's serious disease problems is malaria control. Until recently, malaria was the greatest cause of sickness,

A malaria eradication worker prepares a microscope slide for a blood smear. Looking on are the assistant chief for the zone, standing with clipboard second from right, and his co-worker, Howard Gard, at right. A large part of the program involves visiting villages, on a house-to-house basis.

Howard Gard studies a blood sample in search of the small splotches that indicate malaria. A dozen laboratory workers are kept busy full time at this zone headquarters examining hundreds of slides taken by inspection workers.

debility, and death. The eradication of malaria is a tough, complicated, and challenging job, and the Peace Corps has become deeply involved in the campaign to stamp out the disease.

Volunteers such as Howard Gard (North Sacramento, Calif.) and Victor Hostetter (Los Angeles) became acquainted with rain forests, strange birds, teakwood, wet clothing, rural villages, old logging roads, jeeps, rattan and bamboo thickets, hill climbing, boiled and sticky rice, pickled cucumbers and ginger, betel nuts —and malaria.

Eradication teams pricked fingers by the hundreds for blood smears; they checked children for the telltale sign of a swollen spleen; they treated cases with antimalaria drugs; they prepared public information on malaria prevention and control; they maintained field records.

The first group of Volunteers to work in Thailand's malaria eradication program began early in 1964. The eventual elimination of malaria is so important to the future strength of Thailand's people that the Royal Thai government requested another contingent of Volunteers to expand

Regina Williams, center, a laboratory technician, waits for a blood sample at her laboratory in the Roi-Et Provincial Hospital in northeastern Thailand.

A malaria eradication worker sprays a house with DDT in a village in central Thailand.

and continue the work of the original group.

Thailand also has a pressing need for medical help of another kind. Regina Williams (St. Paul, Minn.), who served as a laboratory technician in the 150-bed Roi-Et Provincial Hospital in the northeastern part of the country, described an unusual feature of hospital life in Thailand:

"Much of the activity of the hospital where I am a laboratory technician goes on not inside the hospital but in a cluster of huts behind it. Here live the patients' relatives.

"I call them 'nurses' aides' for they tend to many of the patients' needs. They are a feature of most hospitals in northeastern Thailand, particularly during the dry season, when there is little to do at home.

"They are quite helpful. They feed, bathe, and comfort the patients, wash their clothes, and visit with them. (Visiting hours are not usually limited in Thai hospitals.)

Mark Hawthorne, a Volunteer English teacher, goes over study materials with Buddhist monks.

Melvin Horwitch (Chicago) teaches English at Mahachulalongkorn Buddhist University in Bangkok.

Marion Hornbeck (Falls Church, Va.) conducts an English class at a teachers' training college at Mahasarakham.

Right, Summer Sharpe (Nashua, N. H.), a city planner, works on a model that he used in classes at Bangkok's Chulalongkorn University.

Bottom, Kermit Krueger (Monitou Beach, Mich.) tries his hand at a local stringed instrument. He taught at a teachers' training college in northeastern Thailand.

"I enjoy watching the women in their *pa-nungs* (sarongs) preparing the charcoal fires to boil rice, and the men in their *pa-ko-mas* (loincloths) carrying water from the hospital well, the tins hanging from a shoulder pole.

"Going to and from the lab, I pass the relatives sitting in the corridors and wards, or under the shade trees, chewing betel nuts, eating sticky rice, and talking.

"In time, as the hospital becomes more conscious of the dangers of contamination, the 'nurses' aides' will probably disappear, replaced by more hygienic, but less interested, attendants."

In contrast to the success of educational and malaria control efforts in Thailand, the Peace Corps has suffered some setbacks in the area of rural community action. Volunteers have often found it difficult to interest villagers in community efforts or even in self-help proposals. Thai villagers seem to be perfectly content with things as they are, which poses a moral question for Thailand's leaders and the Peace Corps. But by any standard some

Standing over a student, Richard Nelson (Brookline, Mass.) monitors an exam at a boys' school in Nakhon Pathom, some thirty miles west of Bangkok. An English teacher, Nelson had twenty-one hours of classes a week. He shared a house about two miles from the school with a Thai teacher and bicycled to work.

Above, Volunteer Victor Hostetter, a malaria eradication worker, checks village visiting charts with a co-worker during a campaign in Thailand's south.

Harley Schwadron (Rockville Centre, N. Y.), a physical education teacher, referees a basketball game in Yala in southern Thailand on the Malay Peninsula.

conditions must be changed: in Thailand, a country heavily dependent upon rice agriculture, there has been no significant increase of rice production in the last thirty years, during which period the population has more than doubled.

Another characteristic of the Thais that causes the Peace Corps difficulty is a tendency to accept authority without question. One factor in this is probably Buddhism, which holds that a person should accept his lot in life as the just

On his way to take an early morning shower, Howard Gard greets a villager from the porch of his quarters.

Above right, Chris Fuges (Philadelphia) assists co-workers in repairing an axle on a heavy truck at a community development center in Ubon in eastern Thailand.

An umbrella maker in the town of Nakhon Pathom.

reward for his conduct. Powerful people or those of high rank are believed to be virtuous *ipso facto*. As a result, inequality is accepted by the Thai more readily than by the Westerner, and so are poverty and ignorance. The Peace Corps must work through the higher, and respected, echelons. Change is unlikely to come from below.

Sam Adams supervises the clearing of heavy jungle for future planting of tea trees in the State of Sabah, formerly North Borneo.

Sam watches one of his Malaysian co-workers lay a bamboo plank floor for a house, one of six he designed and helped build for the tea farm.

Malaysia

On September 16, 1963, the sun set on two more parts of the British Empire as the crown colonies of North Borneo (now called Sabah) and Sarawak joined Singapore State and the Federation of Malaya to form the new nation of Malaysia.

With a majority of Malays and minorities of Chinese, Indians, and others, Malaysia has a population of about 8,000,000. The welter of languages spoken in the country presents problems. Wrote Peter Kramer, a Peace Corps Volunteer from Chicago: "The fantastic diversity of language here surrounds me daily. My fellow teachers speak Panjabi, Bengali, Tamil, Malayalam, Mandarin, Hokkien, Hainanese, Hakka, Cantonese, Malay, and English."

Just north of the equator, Malaysia has a tropical climate. She is the world's greatest producer of rubber and tin, around which her economy centers and which give her the largest per capita in-

Bill Cull, upper left, and villagers complete a water-seal privy behind the home of the imam *(religious leader) of Kampong Sungei Seluang.*

Community development worker Don Mosley (Waco, Tex.) repairs a leak in an earth dam which holds water in a three-acre fishery pond for a government land development program, near Jasin, Malacca State.

come in Southeast Asia. Malaysia's prosperity has been chiefly confined to the cities, where there are hundreds of new schools, office buildings, and paved streets. Well-built highways connect cities and telephones are common. But the roads that go past the *kampongs* (villages) have not appreciably affected rural life. Malaysia has the money to build classrooms and health centers, to buy machinery and heavy equipment, and has spent it. But the more it builds, the more trained people it needs. The Peace Corps is in Malaysia for the ironic reason that it is developing rapidly.

Typical of Peace Corps Volunteers in this country are Bill Cull, an anthropol-

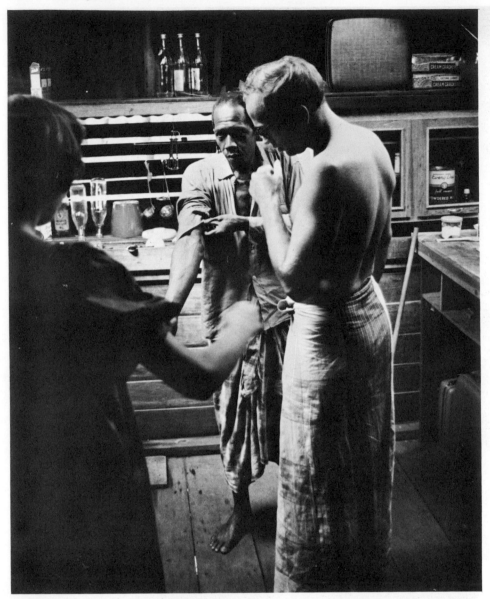

ogist, and his wife, Carol, from Berkeley, California. Engaged in community development, they lived in Kampong Sungei Seluang, a remote village of 500 people in the north. They encouraged and helped the villagers to improve their sanitation facilities and to develop new income and food sources through the establishment of chicken and goat cooperatives. Carol used a small library of paperback books, given by the Peace Corps to all Volunteers, to assist the school children in their study of English. The Culls also provided first-aid services.

Here, as in many countries, local apathy to change and progress had to be fought. Bob Sherman (Freeport, Ill.), who trained heavy-equipment operators on a road project between Kuala Lumpur, the capital, and Ipoh, 110 miles away, described his situation:

"Manual labor was considered undignified. There was no special pride in a job well done, and 'more-money-less-work' seemed to be the motivating force.

"I tried to offset the lack of incentive by

Bill Cull and his wife, Carol, treat a villager's injured hand.

Below left, nurse Sadie Stout (Arkansas City, Kan.) with two young patients at the Sungei Buloh Leprosarium, about forty miles northeast of Kuala Lumpur. A model leprosarium, Sungei Buloh ministers to 2,500 lepers.

Below, Sadie in a ward for the babies of lepers at the Sungei Buloh Leprosarium.

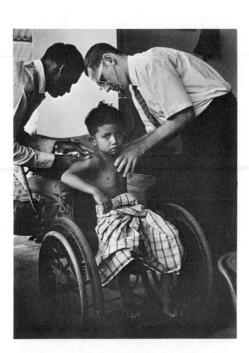

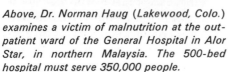

Above, Dr. Norman Haug (Lakewood, Colo.) examines a victim of malnutrition at the out-patient ward of the General Hospital in Alor Star, in northern Malaysia. The 500-bed hospital must serve 350,000 people.

Above right, a Malaysian girl in Jasin, Malacca, enjoys a bowl of wheat provided through the U. S. Food for Peace program.

Judy Baxter (North Providence, R. I.), a nurse, examines an infant while making house calls near Gunong Pasir in Negri Sembilan State. At twenty-three, Judy was in charge of maternity and child health at a rural clinic.

convincing the workers that I would recommend for promotion those who worked hard and showed improvement, and that good operators would be able to find jobs after the Slim River road project was completed. I tried to instill competition and pride in workmanship by designating the 'Number One Operator of the Week.'

"On one exceptionally hot day I offered to spell off one of the operators. Employing various short cuts, I managed to make two trips to one of each of the other Tournapulls [twenty-ton scrapers]. The resting operator studied my actions carefully, and when he climbed back on, he duplicated my demonstration. He has been the 'Number One Operator' ever since."

Special attention is being paid to the development of the State of Sabah. The project of Sam Adams (Huntington, Ind.) is an unusually dramatic example. He spent almost a year clearing off and burning primary jungle and then terracing the

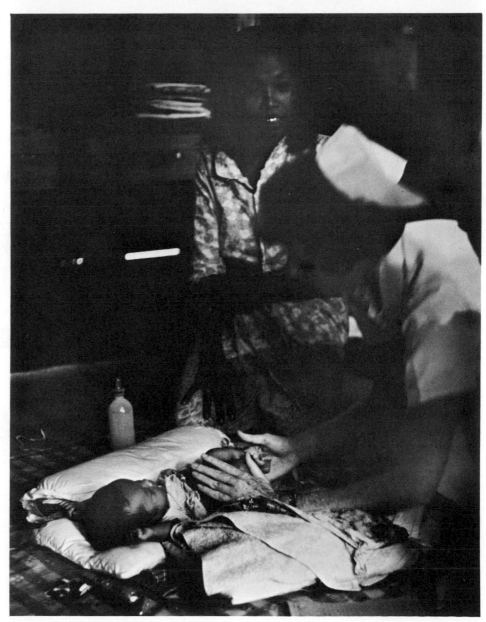

Bill Cull, left, drinks tea with an imam, *right, and two workmen.*

After school, children visit Carol Cull in the small house which their village gave the Culls to live in.

Volunteers in Malaysia find themselves in widely diversified living and working conditions. Although a few carry on their work in an air-conditioned atmosphere, some are leading what must be called "the simple life." A report depicting such life came from an engineer who had designed and built himself a convenience:

"Worried lest a tidal wave inundate my lavatory, the platform was designed to a total height of 38 feet 6¼ inches above ground level. It was decided to clothe the structure in shiny galvanized corrugated metal. The resulting façade is something that brings a tear to the eye of an engineer, and even an architect would have to admit that there is something intrinsically wrong with the design.

"I live in fear that the structure will be struck by lightning. This might be a blessing, except that it would be just my luck to be in it at the time. As it is now, the latrine is a landmark, and planes have been known to circle over it, presumably to get a fix on their bearings or possibly to get aerial photos of what may look from the air like a rocket shed."

steep hillsides of this mountainous area for the planting of tea trees. The place where he worked had no name; it was commonly called "the Mile 33 on the Sensuron Track." It was an eleven-mile walk, 4,500 feet down to the road.

Africa

In January, 1965, Nigeria received her thirteenth shipment of Peace Corps teachers. The 105 men and women in this group had trained at U.C.L.A. and were about to disperse to secondary schools in every part of Africa's most populous nation. Their arrival in Lagos, the clamorous port capital, could hardly have been considered an earth-shattering event. In slightly over three years of participation, Nigeria had ceased to look on the Peace Corps as a novelty. Later in the year, in May and September, two more groups were scheduled to land in Lagos. Nevertheless, the Honorable Alhaji Waziri Ibrahim, Nigeria's Minister of Education and Economic Development, did not consider the coming of the thirteenth group a purely routine matter. He went out to welcome the new arrivals in person.

"Five years ago," Ibrahim told them, "when the idea of the Peace Corps was first mooted, some nations had their misgivings and therefore hesitated to ask for Peace Corps assistance. In Nigeria at that time, we felt that our needs in the field of education were very great. We therefore had no hesitation in asking for Peace Corps Volunteers in the fields of modern languages, science, and mathematics. Since then, 1,025 Peace Corps Volunteers have come to this country to teach in our schools. Not less than 530 are in the field today, excluding the 105 here this morning. . . .

"This corps of Volunteers has contributed immensely to the training of our youths in secondary schools and teacher training colleges. They have enriched school life by a wide variety of extracurricular activities. They have organized libraries. They have given radio lessons. They have created science laboratories. They have produced plays. They have brought a new dimension to physical education in our land. They have led school excursions. They have undertaken research in local history. What is more—they have identified themselves with the future progress of their pupils in such a manner that lasting friendships have been formed.

"It is no exaggeration to say that today many Nigerians, whose faith in the United States was badly shaken by the assassination of President Kennedy, have recovered their equilibrium as a result of the friendship and humanity of the Americans working in our midst. Many of our children have identified Americans with Peace Corps Volunteers and their enthusiasm. I can therefore state without any fear of contradiction that the image of America has been greatly enhanced by the Peace Corps Volunteers who have worked with us. Those of you coming here for the first time have the privilege of contributing to a record that is already impressive and fully appreciated."

These complimentary words were a long way from the mood of some Nigerians in November, 1961, when a now almost-forgotten incident over a post card threatened to send the Peace Corps packing before the first Volunteers in Nigeria had even gone to work. Volunteer Margery Michelmore had been in the country less than two weeks and was taking orientation training at the University of Ibadan before setting out for her teaching assignment. On her way to the post office one morning she inadvertently dropped a post card on the street. The card was found by Nigerian students from the University who decided that it contained statements insulting to their country. The card's contents were widely publicized, and before the episode was over Miss Michelmore returned home. The tension did not evaporate until the rest of her group went to work and Nigerians had a chance to see what the Peace Corps' true intentions were.

Since then, as Minister Ibrahim pointed out, more than a thousand Volunteer teachers have served in Nigeria. Most of them were assigned to secondary schools, where elementary school teachers are trained; a few were sent to universities. Volunteers were similarly assigned in the big Peace Corps teach-

ing program in Ethiopia. Malawi and Liberia became the scenes of elementary school programs in addition to secondary school teaching. Volunteers were sent to teach in the secondary schools of still other African nations where English is the language of instruction: Kenya, Uganda, Somalia, and Tanzania (formerly Tanganyika and Zanzibar) in the east; Ghana and Sierra Leone in the west. Teaching programs were also mounted in seven French-speaking nations of sub-Saharan Africa—Cameroon, Niger, Togo, Ivory Coast, Guinea, Gabon, and Senegal—as well as in Tunisia and Morocco.

Not all Volunteers sent to Africa are teachers. Tanzania asked for and received surveyors, engineers, and nurses. Medical and public health programs were organized in Sierra Leone, Togo, and Ethiopia. School construction teams were assigned to Gabon. Architects and heavy-equipment operators and repairmen went to Tunisia. Agriculture programs were established in Morocco, Senegal, and Guinea. Ghana received a geological survey team. Law experts were sent to Liberia, Nigeria, and Ethiopia. Fishery experts were sent to Togo. New programs for Africa are constantly being developed outside the domain of teaching.

Nevertheless, Africa and teaching are almost synonymous as far as the Peace Corps is concerned. In the years since World War II, the world has witnessed the dramatic spectacle of Africa's release from colonialism. History, the times, and the Africans themselves demanded independence, and there was no delaying it. Yet Africa's proud new nations were the first to admit that their needs in education were desperate. The shortage of teachers was so critical in parts of Africa that there seemed little chance of producing more: the number of children getting an education might be so small that few could be spared for teaching. African nations set out to get teachers wherever they could be obtained. Education costs made up huge percentages of national budgets in many new nations. But because these nations were new, budget limitations were usually severe. For much of Africa, the Peace Corps was a godsend.

In Ethiopia, not a new nation but an old one now embarked on the path of industrial development, the first contingent of Peace Corps teachers doubled the capacity of the secondary schools. In Ghana, a mere sixty Volunteer teachers in their first year offered at least one course to half of the nation's secondary school students. Peace Corps teachers in the whole of Africa constitute the largest overseas educational program in history—and it will get larger before it gets smaller. Africa will eventually have produced enough teachers of its own, and the help of Peace Corps Volunteers will no longer be needed.

Meanwhile, they will continue with this huge task, generally as unglamorous as it is compellingly necessary. Volunteer teachers in Africa go off to their classes and their other duties each day in a routine as fixed as it is for teachers in, say, Cincinnati. They have discipline problems with high-spirited and occasionally obstreperous students. They form friendships with the young people they see daily, and they often feel torn at parting when their two years are up and they return to the United States. They keep in touch by letter long after they have returned; some of these correspondences will last lifetimes.

Many African schools, such as the secondary schools of Ghana, are handsome, modern, and well equipped. Other African schools are a long way from the schools of Cincinnati. In some of them, the Volunteer teachers must improvise everything—blackboards, writing equipment, textbooks. Some of the Volunteer teachers have taught before; most have not. In any case, all of them must adjust to unfamiliar ways of doing things and school systems modeled usually on the systems of Britain or France. Some are assigned to cities—Dakar, Abidjan, Nairobi—where every amenity is available. Many more are assigned to the provincial capitals where life is stretched and suspended between the industrial world and the African past. Still others are teaching deep in the rain forests that line the Bight of Benin, or on the rain-drenched slopes of volcanic Cameroon Mountain, or in Niger's endlessly arid distances of sun and sand, or on the mountain-ringed Ethiopian highlands.

And so there they are in Africa, a few thousand Peace Corps teachers from every state in the union, men and women, as young as eighteen, as old as seventy-five. No statistics can convey the scope of their separate experiences nor measure what they have done to bring Africa and America closer together. Some of the feeling of one location was conveyed in a letter from Anabel Leinbach (Reading, Pa.), who was just twenty-one when she arrived to teach school in Cameroon. Her school was the Women's Teacher Training College in the Mankon section of the Bamenda highlands.

"The mountains are everywhere—green, high, and jagged. When the rains come, green volcanoes feign eruption in the life of the waters. The wind of the dry season, the *harmattan*, envelops everything in dust—even the mountains.

"The school doesn't sit like any other school; it rests in its own valley. . . . The big rains rush over from the mountains; you run to beat them and in flooded classrooms shout to outdo the pounding on the tin roofs.

"It is a joy to fight life and to sleep from exhaustion to the sound of chant and drums."

Mary Rightmire and Virginia Wolfe stroll through the Lalla Mimouna souk, or outdoor market, shopping for meat and vegetables.

Mary shows a Moroccan woman how to operate a sewing machine in the adult education and child care center, in Lalla Mimouna.

Morocco

A hot, dusty hamlet with the muscial name of Lalla Mimouna, deep inside Morocco, was the home for many months of two American girls, Virginia Wolfe (Cleveland, Ohio) and Mary Rightmire (Bryn Mawr, Pa.), during their Peace Corps career in this North African country. Lalla Mimouna is one of several pilot villages that the Moroccan government has selected for settling nomadic people of the *bled*, or interior. The nomads are moved from grass hovels on the flat, parched countryside to more permanent homes in the villages.

Teaching English in Fez, a large inland city, was Mary and Virginia's primary assignment in Morocco, but the government asked the girls to help run an adult education and child care center in Lalla Mimouna as a vacation project. Although no foreigner had lived in the village before and its only connection with the civilized world was a single daily taxi run, the Volunteers accepted the invitation.

Adult education centers are an essential feature of the resettlement program. Women, accustomed to the passivity and seclusion of Moslem tradition, are asked to make a break with the past by attending homemaking classes. In Lalla Mimouna, Mary and Virginia opened their center each morning to teach sewing on the handful of machines with which the village had been equipped. Timid mothers, whose attendance was erratic, were asked to make twenty-five yellow jumpers for the children who went to the center to learn games and songs. The mothers advanced slowly and only a few of the jumpers were ever finished, but the Volunteers felt that the mere act of attending classes had loosened ancient constraints and, if followed by other programs, would eventually have a stimulating effect on the community's welfare.

English was unknown in the village.

Outside the center Virginia Wolfe teaches youngsters the game of London Bridge.

Virginia, left, and Mary take tea and cookies with the village grocer. They conversed in French.

A *bidonville, or "tin-can villa,"* in Rabat, Morocco's capital.

A father and his son who live in a Moroccan bidonville.

Only one person, the grocer, spoke French. Arabic, the language of Morocco, was difficult for the two Americans, who suffered occasional attacks of loneliness. Shopping had to be done at the weekly *souk*, or outdoor market, which was set up in a grove of trees, and water had to be hauled from a distant spring. In spite of their isolation and hardships Mary and Virginia could say at the end of six months, "It's been the best time of our lives, and the freest. The people were extraordinarily generous and kind."

Morocco has played host to several hundred Volunteers. In addition to teachers, the Peace Corps has sent athletic instructors, surveyors, foresters, and agriculture extension agents to the staunchly independent kingdom. Some Volunteers are stationed in remote desert country; others are assigned to cities, like Casablanca and Rabat, the capital, where large numbers of Europeans live.

The tradition-bound country has proved especially challenging to Volunteers. Frederick C. Thomas, Peace Corps Representative in Morocco until July, 1964, reported, "Wherever they are [in Morocco] Volunteers come up against factors which inhibit the fulfillment of their mission. Moroccans are a proud people

In Rabat, a veil-covered woman passes a wall papered over by flashy advertisements.

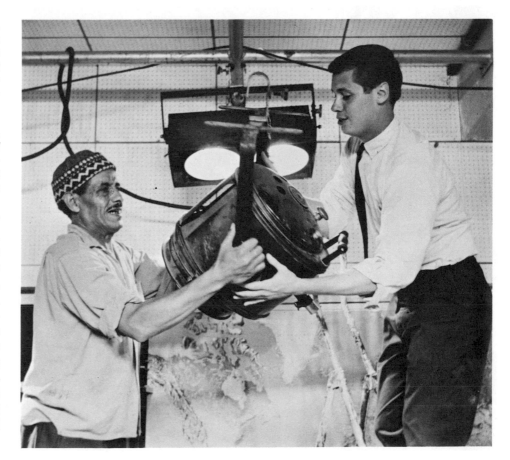

At a camp on the Atlantic coast north of Rabat, Bill Hammatt (Anaheim, Calif.) and Bob Bartlett (Salem, Ore.) give a swimming lesson in light surf. The two Volunteers, who taught physical education at an inland school, devoted their summers to counseling in the seaside children's camp.

Before the start of a television show in Rabat, Gordon L. Schimmel (Battle Creek, Mich.) and a Moroccan lighting technician prepare equipment. Schimmel was an English teacher but spent his summers working in television studios.

with a long history of independence. . . . When the Peace Corps began, there was some doubt that the Volunteers were really needed or wanted. Officially, yes, but at the working level, perhaps not. . . .

"It is obvious that Morocco is a difficult country in which to measure Peace Corps accomplishment. Nevertheless, the Peace Corps—or rather individual Peace Corps Volunteers—in a highly individualistic and personal society have exercised an important influence in their schools and communities, both in terms of practical results and psychological impact."

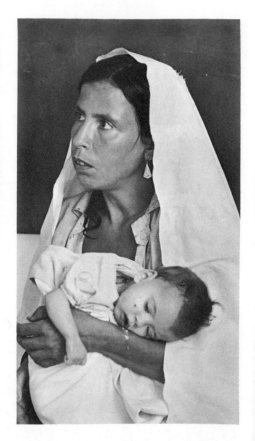

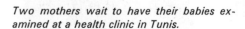

Two mothers wait to have their babies examined at a health clinic in Tunis.

At the clinic, nurse Margaret Gallen fills her hypodermic with water to arrest a baby's dehydration. At left is a Tunisian nurse's aide, whom Peggy helped to train.

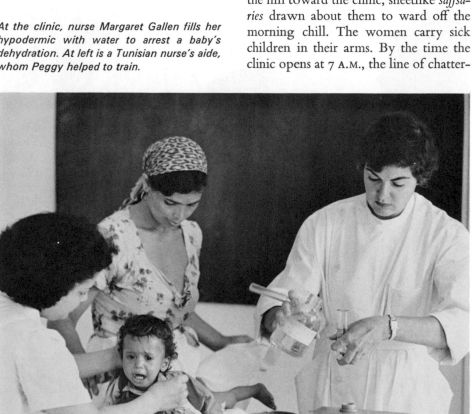

beneath the ruins of a fortress built centuries ago by the Spaniards. At sunup every day Bedouin mothers start down the hill toward the clinic, sheetlike *saffsaries* drawn about them to ward off the morning chill. The women carry sick children in their arms. By the time the clinic opens at 7 A.M., the line of chattering, arguing women stretches a block long.

The clinic is run by the World Health Organization. An average of two hundred babies a day are treated there. Almost all suffer from malnutrition, and many are victims of acute dehydration brought on by diarrhea. For nearly two years, Margaret Gallen (Philadelphia, Pa.) worked there as a nurse.

Peggy carried on a quiet but relentless fight to get liquid into her young patients. Every morning she boiled up a mixture of rice and salt water, which she sent back up the hill in bottles. There was enough water in each bottle to keep a child's liquid intake at the right level for twenty-four hours. However, some children required a painful but necessary emergency treatment: direct injection of water by means of a hypodermic needle.

Another program of major importance sponsored by the Tunisian government is community development. Perhaps no other country in the world takes town planning and slum clearance as seriously as Tunisia, which has requested help from international organizations and from countries both Eastern and Western. Peace Corps architects found themselves working shoulder-to-shoulder with Italians and Bulgarians, as well as Tunisians.

Young American architects, some of whom had just finished their training, designed 144 projects between 1962 and 1964, including 27 schools, 15 low-income housing developments, and a complete, new community on the outskirts of Tunis.

A member of the first group of architects to go to Tunisia, David Hanchett (Ticonderoga, N. Y.), helped design a self-contained, Moorish-style community for twenty-five hundred people, consisting of five hundred two-room living units and schools, markets, and wells. Lowell Sykes (Idaho Falls, Ida.) was a general foreman on a project in Souk-el-Arba, an agricultural community of 30,000 people

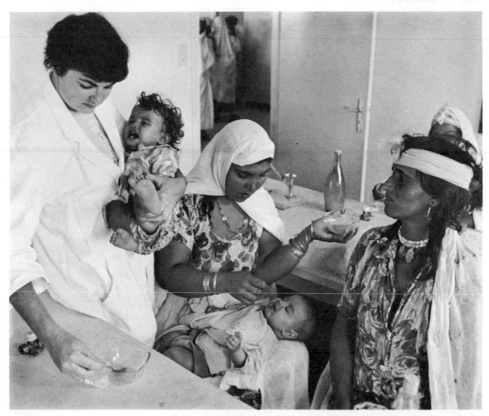

Nurse Gallen shows a mother how to get liquid into her dehydrated baby, while another mother, center, spoons water into her baby's mouth.

Outside the clinic Peggy stops to admire a youngster dressed like her mother in flowing headdress.

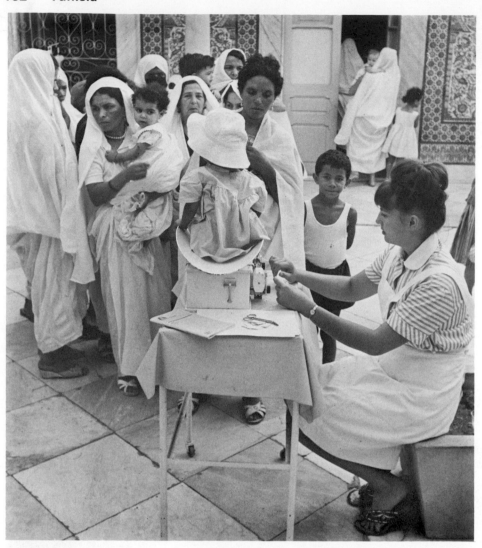

west of Tunis. He supervised the building of a fourteen-room schoolhouse as part of his work.

The experiences of Stuart W. McKenzie and his wife, Carolyn, from Grandview, Washington, were different from those of other Volunteers who worked in the more developed parts of this ancient and not unsophisticated country. Stuart taught new agricultural methods in Ouled M'Hamed, an experimental farm of four thousand acres, deep in the interior, just a few miles from the empty wastes of the Sahara. Only nine inches of rain falls yearly there, and so the fields of almonds, olives, cotton, corn, hay, peanuts, barley, vetch, peas, and beans must be irrigated.

Like impoverished farmers the world over, the eleven hundred Arab tribesmen at Ouled M'Hamed were conservative and reluctant to give up traditional modes of agriculture. McKenzie said, "When I first suggested that they put up vetch and barley silage for their livestock, they said, 'No, no, God will take care of our cows.' I persuaded them to give it a try anyway,

Mothers line up to have their babies weighed at a small clinic in Tunis. At the scales is Sandy Ketner (Kansas City, Kan.).

Christine Krutenat (Webster, N. Y.) makes a post-surgical check of a ward patient in a Tunis hospital.

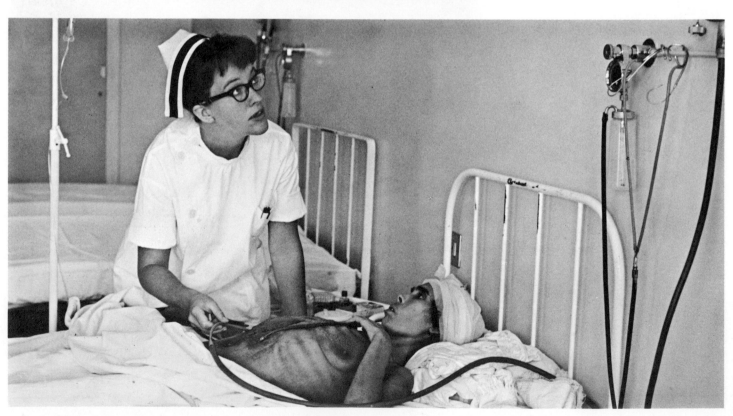

Stuart McKenzie, in white shirt at rear, stands by as his crew brings in a crop of silage at Ouled M'Hamed.

McKenzie shares a joke with Bedouin workmen who are digging an irrigation ditch.

and when they saw how fat their cattle were becoming on silage they became very enthusiastic. Now they can't wait for this year's crop."

One of the many architects that the Peace Corps has sent to Tunisia was Jacques Ullman (Portola Valley, Calif.), who graduated from the University of California in Berkeley. He described the unusual position of the Peace Corps in Tunisia:

"I suspect that Tunisia is rather an atypical Peace Corps country in that it has a well-established bourgeoisie. Tunis has its traffic jams, night clubs, and cafés. The Twist and Bossa Nova are common. Office workers are expected to wear a tie and a clean shirt to work, and owning an automobile is in no way unusual. In other words, there is no question of our living in grass huts. So what is a Peace Corps Volunteer doing here? He is here to work and set an example."

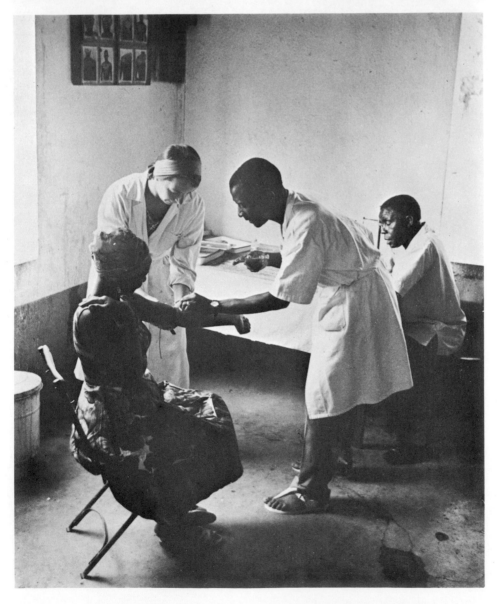

Guinea

With some of the world's largest deposits of bauxite, with diamonds, gold, and iron ore, and with coffee, bananas, palm nuts, and pineapples, Guinea should be a wealthy nation. However, her mineral wealth is unexploited to its full advantage and agricultural production, which occupies 90 per cent of Guinea's 3,000,000 people, has sagged recently.

The typical Guinean farmer ekes out a living by clearing jungle from his tiny plot of ground and then coaxing spindly plants from the hard, red earth. Rarely do meat and green vegetables find their way into the family cooking pot. Many children mature poorly or weaken and die from the monotonously starchy diet, which is almost totally lacking in protein.

Peace Corps Volunteers in this former West African French territory work in medical, industrial, and agricultural projects.

The Guinean government has given high priority to agricultural development. Volunteers have been sent into the countryside to augment the production of livestock, to introduce poultry raising, and to increase yields of Guinea's major export crops.

In September, 1958, Guinea opted out of the French Community. An abrupt withdrawal of all French monetary assistance and technical aid ensued and Guinea was forced to look to other nations for help.

Top, an accomplished musician, Linda Mintener (Minneapolis, Minn.), the wife of Brad Mintener, one of the Peace Corps staff members in Guinea, teaches flute at the National School of Music in Conakry, the capital.

Left, in a leprosarium in the interior town of Dabola, Mary Lou Callahan (Vermilion, Ohio) helps a local medical technician give a leper a periodic shot. Mary Lou was an English teacher, but during the rainy-season vacation she helped out in the local leprosarium.

Opposite top left, two mothers and their children outside their stone and thatched hut in the Fouta Djallon mountains.

Opposite top right, in the leprosarium, Mary Lou Callahan is shown how to use a microscope by a Guinean laboratory technician.

Right, Mary Lou gives a patient his monthly pills at the Dabola leprosarium.

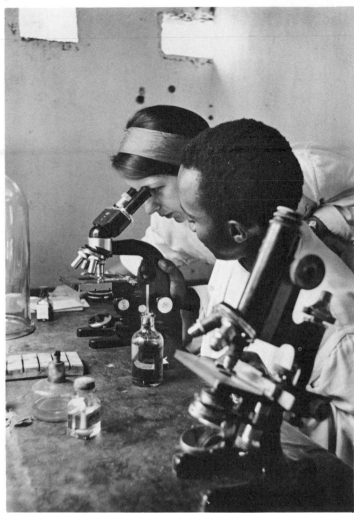

Ghana

In September, 1961, the first Peace Corps Volunteers arrived in Ghana. Fifty-one young American men and women came to teach in the secondary schools of the former British colony, which had gained her full independence only four years earlier.

These Volunteers, the first to go to any country, had been given only two months of language training. When they got off the plane and sang a song in Twi, the commonest of Ghana's many languages, their pronunciation was less than perfect. But their song was a hit and so were they. Before the end of the first year, half the secondary school students in the country had come into contact with Peace Corps teachers.

By late 1964, Volunteers in Ghana were teaching in more than sixty schools containing over 40 per cent of all secondary

---

Top, Marian Frank (Pittsburgh, Pa.) smiles at the enthusiastic participation of her French class at the Yaa Asantewa Girls' School in Kumasi.

Left, Michael Shea (Eau Claire, Wis.), at the secondary school in Kibi.

Kenneth Baer (Beverly Hills, Calif.) taught at the Ebeneezer School in Accra, the capital. Below left, students group around him after class. Below, he helps out one of the students with his problems.

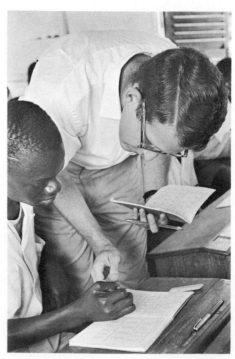

school students and plans were completed to send even more Peace Corps teachers to the country. The subjects most frequently taught are mathematics, science, and French.

Formerly called the Gold Coast, Ghana is a West African country of over 7,000,000 people with an area of 91,843 square miles. Ghana's 334-mile coast line consists mostly of low, sandy shore, behind which stretches the coastal plain. A forest belt extends northward from the western coast for about 170 miles before joining an area of steep ridges and thick woods. The climate is tropical.

Ghana is rich in mineral wealth, including manganese, gold, diamonds, and bauxite. Forest reserves are great and cocoa is grown extensively. Educators and technicians are needed to help Ghana get started on the road to a modern economy.

A Volunteer described life in Ghana's ambitious educational program:

"All but seven of our group of fifty-one teach in boarding schools operated on the English system. Most of these are built on one master plan, consisting of pastel stucco classroom blocks, dormitories, and four-room staff bungalows spaced over a square mile of cleared brush. Most are located on the outskirts of a small town in the rain forest or on the coastal plains. . . .

"Some [teachers] have their subject matter and classroom schedule rigidly prescribed. Others have had to start from scratch, even, in the case of science, deciding which science to teach, ordering textbooks, and writing their own syllabi. Some with heavy dormitory duties inspect beds at 6:30 A.M., supervise nap hour, athletics, homework periods at night, washing, and Sunday church services. I personally had an impossible time keeping track of pocket money for ninety-three girls. . . .

"Whatever the specific conditions, these schools all demand more creativity and on-the-spot resourcefulness than schools at home. They demand a sixth sense to know when to assume command of a situation and when to quietly sit back and learn."

Top, Ophelia DeLaine (Hollis, N. Y.), a teacher of biology, and her students at Opoku Ware school in Kumasi.

Deliberating a purchase, Dorothy Vellenga (New Concord, Ohio), a teacher, shops in the market in Accra.

Ethiopia

With the exception of Liberia and Egypt, Ethiopia, in east central Africa, is the oldest independent state on the continent. Tradition credits the founding of Ethiopia to the first son of King Solomon by the Queen of Sheba, around 1,000 B.C. Records, however, only go back to the first century A.D. Christianity in Ethiopia has ancient roots: the Coptic Church has been there since the fourth century. Today, over one half of Ethiopia's population of 22,000,000 still practices Christianity.

Ethiopia is the only African nation ever to have defeated a European force. In 1896, at the battle of Aduwa, she turned back a large invading Italian force.

Gertrude Solomon massages the foot of a polio patient in Dessye. The boy's mother sought out Miss Solomon in the market place —her son had never walked. Nurse Solomon discovered the boy had polio and began treatment. The boy was fitted with braces and was soon able to take his first step.

Dennis Fox conducts an ancient history class at a school in Yirga-Alam that serves as a secondary school for all of Sidamo-Borano province.

The "Lion of Judah," Haile Selassie I, Emperor since 1930, is well known for his valiant stand against Mussolini before and during the Second World War. Forced to withdraw in 1936, he returned to the throne in 1941.

Past glories, preserved traditions, pressing economic and social problems—these make up the heritage of the modern Ethiopian who, although he belongs to a civilization that goes back to the beginning of history, is forced to start from the beginning in building schools and hospitals, modernizing old crafts, and constructing factories, dams, and industries.

Located on a plateau with an average elevation of eight thousand feet, Ethiopea is a land of vast potential, with great natural resources of hydroelectric power, minerals, and fertile soil (some of the best

Alice Sprengle demonstrates proper food preparation to one of her students in a secondary school in Jimma, a town 150 miles southwest of Addis Ababa, the capital.

Below right, Dr. Anna Browder makes friends with a young mother and her baby in a hospital in Dessye.

A proud old Ethiopian.

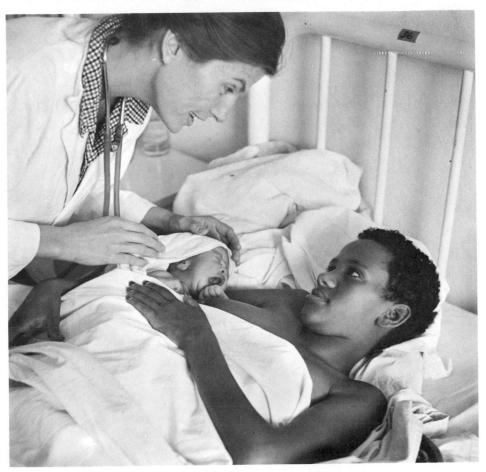

Russell Berman talks with one of the many Ethiopian officials he worked with at the Institute of Public Administration in Addis Ababa.

Youngsters surround Daryle Russel in Addis Ababa. He obtained permission from the city government to close the street on which they are standing and convert it into a playground.

coffee in the world is grown on the pleasant plateau and mountains of the Kaffa province). To take advantage of what nature has given her, Ethiopia needs help in educating a generation of people.

With one million children of secondary school age, only one child in eight was enrolled in school before the first Peace

A young Ethiopian girl.

Corps contingent arrived. The Ethiopian Ministry of Education and Fine Arts is increasing the number of elementary and secondary schools, but until a sufficient number of Ethiopian teachers have been trained, the Ministry must rely extensively on Peace Corps teachers. At the higher level, nearly 45 per cent of all teachers are American men and women.

In Harar, a town in the eastern section of the country, so many Ethiopian children wanted to study with the Americans that there were not enough classrooms to accommodate them—a promising situation in a land sometimes plagued by apathy. An inspection disclosed a school that had been abandoned because it was old and falling apart. The Volunteers persuaded the town to repair the school as a community project and persuaded the government to foot the bills. The cost: $380. It is now known as Model School Number Two and serves more than three hundred children in the primary grades.

Volunteers such as Dennis Fox (Philadelphia, Pa.), who conducted history classes in the Ras Dasta primary and secondary school in Yirga-Alam in the Great Rift Valley to the south; Daryle Russel (Portland, Ore.), who was athletic director at Haile Selassie I University; home economics teacher Alice Sprengle (Steamboat Springs, Colo.), who taught at a secondary school in Jimma in the

Mary Leonard shows her laboratory assistant the proper use of a microscope.

Alfred Hartwell, left, and Floyd Davis walk down a street in Gore, where Hartwell taught English and Davis biology and chemistry.

Below, Floyd Davis conducts an outdoor question-and-answer session in Gore.

southwest—all tackled the strenuous daily schedule of teaching combined with involvement in their communities. Teachers Alfred Hartwell (Honolulu) and Floyd Davis (South Norwalk, Conn.), teaching in the town of Gore, situated at an altitude of 6,580 feet in southwestern Ethiopia, had to fly once a month to the capital, Addis Ababa, to buy their groceries, since there are no roads into Gore. Russell Berman (Chicago), a Harvard Law School graduate, helped draft laws, codify them, and draft bills for the Prime Minister.

Ethiopia has also made good use of Peace Corps doctors and medical technicians. The Peace Corps dispatched Dr. Anna Browder (Hackettstown, N. J.), a graduate of The Johns Hopkins University, to a ninety-bed hospital in the northeastern town of Dessye, where she served as director and administrator and doctor for fifty to sixty outpatients a day. Also sent to Dessye were nurse Gertrude Solomon (Tarzana, Calif.), who had worked for thirteen years at the Los Angeles General Hospital, and Mary Leonard (Spokane, Wash.), a medical technician.

Cameroon

The Federal Republic of Cameroons in West Africa faced a real crisis, owing to a shortage of trained teachers, engineers, surveyors, and other skilled personnel, a year after it won its independence in 1960. The new nation, somewhat smaller than Sweden and with a population of about 4,500,000, today consists of what was formerly the French Cameroons and the southern half of the British Cameroons. When the merger took place in 1961, most of the French and British teachers, technicians, and civil servants left the country. As a result, many schools were forced to close; others continued with skeleton staffs and school instruction lagged.

Al Scarborough (Pedricktown, N. J.), a community development worker, helps the villagers of Mamfe in West Cameroon in the construction of a road he traced through the raw bush terrain.

Below left, a Volunteer discusses the operation of a road grader with a Cameroonian co-worker. He is Harry Haywood (Taberg, N.Y.), who, as a heavy-equipment maintenance man, worked with rural development workers in Bamenda, West Cameroon.

Below, Ed Douglass (Appleton, Wis.), a teacher at the Ombe Technical Training Center near Victoria, West Cameroon, helps his students with some electrical installation at the school. In addition to his teaching activities, he helped and supervised students on school construction projects.

At the request of the Cameroon Prime Minister, the Peace Corps first sent a large number of teachers and later a smaller number of community development workers to help fill the void. Most of the schools in which Volunteers teach are run by Presbyterian, Baptist, or Roman Catholic missions but are largely directed and financially supported by the government.

Reviewing the progress that these Volunteers have made, A. D. Mengot, Director of Education for West Cameroon, observed, "Their arrival has permitted us to open new secondary and teacher training schools and greatly expand the enrollment of existing ones."

Volunteer teachers are expected to engage in extracurricular work, such as participating in school construction projects and organizing sports and community recreational programs, during their free hours. In the coastal town of Kribi, for example, a teacher, Carl Stinson (Bath, Me.), organized a fishing cooperative to enable the fishermen to sell their catches in the large city of Douala, nearly one hundred miles away.

Willie Wilkerson (Naylor, Ga.), right, inspects masonry work on a school construction job. Wilkerson was a teacher at the Ombe Technical Training Center.

Below, Carl Stinson, a teacher who organized a fishing cooperative in the coastal village of Kribi in West Cameroon, helps the local fishermen untangle their lines and pull in their nets.

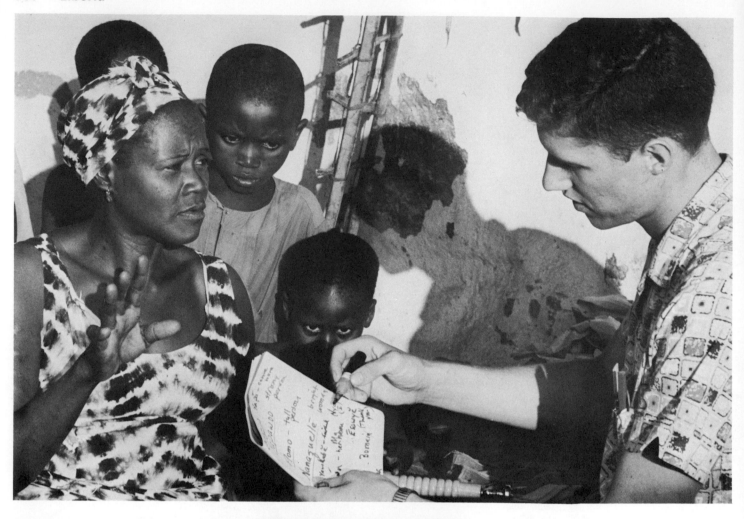

Liberia

Liberia, the oldest independent republic in Africa, was founded in 1822 by former American slaves. Under the sponsorship of the American Colonization Society, freed men from the United States set up the colony of Monrovia, named in honor of President James Monroe. Liberia became a republic in 1847, with Monrovia as its capital. The country now has a population of about 2,500,000.

The official language is English, though a variety of languages and dialects is spoken. Teaching of English is stressed in the more than seven hundred schools that are scattered throughout the country—but there has been a shortage of teachers to carry out the needs. The Peace Corps

Top, teacher David Smith (Seattle, Wash.) practices the Kpelle language with a Liberian woman. Kpelle is one of a variety of dialects spoken in Liberia.

An arithmetic class is conducted by Kiyo Massengale (San Luis Obispo, Calif.), in the coastal town of River Cess.

Fascinated by their visitor, Liberian women and children crowd around Carol Smith (Marysville, Wash.), an English teacher, as she strolls through their village.

Living grass roots-style, teacher Lois Hirst (Miamisburg, Ohio) irons clothes with a coal iron, while a young Liberian stops to watch her. Other garments dry on the lines behind her.

has responded to the government's request for trained educators.

In September, 1963, 114 teachers and 45 public administrators joined the first two groups of Volunteers in Liberia. The public administration group was a pilot project, the first Volunteers to fill jobs within the government of a foreign nation. These public administrators work in twelve government departments. Included in the variety of jobs are those of assistant hospital administrator, archives clerk in the State Department, assistant to a district commissioner, assistant to a district road-maintenance engineer, assistant manager of an agricultural research center, and reporter for the Liberian Information Service.

Mario J. DiSanto (Brooklyn, N. Y.) and his crew struggle with heavy cement drainage pipes for a road in Daru, a remote village in the extreme southeastern section of Sierra Leone. Among many other hazards, DiSanto and his crew had to stay on the alert for poisonous snakes.

Below, a Sierra Leone boy and a Mendi mother and child.

Sierra Leone

A former British colony in West Africa and now one of the smaller independent states on the continent, Sierra Leone is a hilly, fertile, and well-watered tropical land, whose economy is mainly based on such items as palm kernels, coffee, cocoa, kola nuts, and ginger.

Community development and construction have high priorities on the Peace Corps' program list in Sierra Leone. Road building, a next-to-impossible task because of alternating extreme wet and dry seasons, has occupied several Volunteers. School construction claims the time of many others.

One imaginative Volunteer, Tim Howell (Raytown, Mo.), hit upon the idea of an A-frame design for a school he was planning to build. The idea was suggested to him by the shape of *shimbeks*, little shelters of thatch and poles that Sierra Leone farmers sleep under while they are out in the fields harvesting crops. Such was the appeal of the A-frame to the village in which Howell worked that local people eagerly volunteered to help build the school and later decided to build houses of the same design.

Opposite top, Bill Atkins (Rockland, Mass.) and his construction crew take shelter from the rain, which falls almost incessantly for six months out of the year. Atkins was a community development worker who helped to build schools.

Right, Jack Chapman (Seaside, Ore.), in white shirt, center, works with a road-building crew near the town of Bo. Sierra Leone men are required to donate thirty days a year to public works projects.

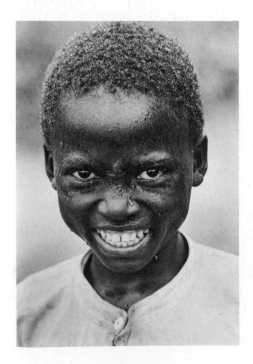

Nigeria

"We are here because there's a job to do. We are sacrificing nothing except a few amenities we can nicely do without.... We are teaching and we are learning."

The author of these words is one of a contingent of Peace Corps Volunteer teachers in Nigeria who are teaching near

Top, Mrs. Dorothy Payne, sixty-six, conducts an English class at the Federal Advanced Teachers College outside Lagos, the capital. She and her husband, Dr. Virgil Payne, sixty-seven, were the oldest couple in the Peace Corps in June, 1964. The Paynes are from Little Silver, New Jersey.

Left, at the Moor Plantation experimental farm in western Nigeria, Don Ferguson (Salem, N. Y.), holds a Holstein so that a blood smear can be drawn to see if the cow has been bitten by tsetse flies.

Opposite top, observed closely by a Nigerian student, Dr. Virgil Payne conducts an experiment in his chemistry class at the Federal Advanced Teachers College outside Lagos.

Right, Lucy Wallace (Mound, Minn.) teaches a class in French at the University of Ife in Ibadan. She was head of the French department.

Far right, the first Peace Corps baby born overseas, Robin Adesode (Nigerian for "born away from home") is shown with her parents, teachers David and Judy Danielson, at their home on the campus of Edo College in Benin City, in 1963. David wears a Nigerian wrapper. The Danielson family now lives in Boston, Massachusetts.

On a shopping tour, teacher Natalia Forsyth (Hubbard, Ohio) looks over the wares in the market square in Enugu, where her school was located.

Elin Yougdahl (Wrentham, Mass.) joins two of her students in a mango-sampling session on the Ibadan campus of the University of Ife.

the coast, where school compounds are sometimes in the midst of a tropical rain forest; in teeming cities, where there are modern buildings and where an African version of rock and roll blares in the night; in the northern region, where there are ancient cities and camel trains begin long treks across the desert.

Nigeria, a former British colony, is a vast country, with an area of more than 350,000 square miles. It is the most populous nation in Africa—55,000,000. At its southernmost point it lies four degrees north of the equator.

The Peace Corps was invited to Nigeria in 1961, about a year after the country gained independence, and in January, 1965, had about six hundred Volunteers on the job. This was primarily a secondary school and university education program and it remained so until the arrival in 1964 of groups trained in agriculture and community development. There are

Carrying a bucket of mud Nigeria-style, teacher Marston Hodgin (Oxford, Ohio) helps workmen in the building of an incinerator on Marako Island.

Two Volunteers from Niger are guests for breakfast at the home of Jacqueline Taylor (Blue River, Ore.), center, in Bichi. Jacqueline and Bill Melvin (Independence, Iowa), right, were both on the faculty of the Bichi Teacher Training College.

also small groups of Volunteer lawyers and secretaries. The Volunteers work in all five of Nigeria's universities and in nearly two hundred secondary schools and teacher training colleges all over the country.

Soon after Martin Gleason (Chicago) returned home after concluding his Peace Corps service in Nigeria, where he taught law at the University of Nigeria, he received a letter from one of his law students, Lawrence Okwuosa:

"The Peace Corps venture I take as the greatest attempt at restoring understanding between people of this country and the U. S. These men and women have done a duty which gold and dollar have failed to accomplish. Gold and dollar have each attempted this through aid but failed because they failed to find the real human need. . . ."

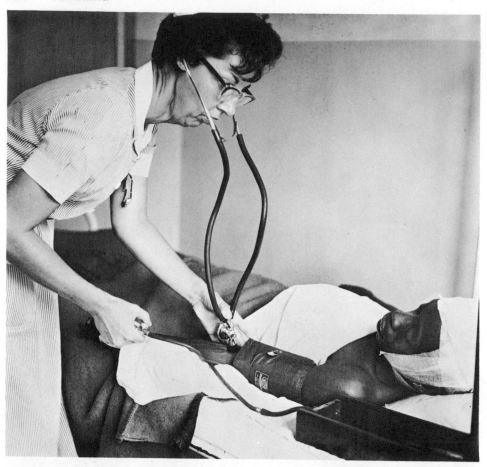

Tanzania

In 1964 a new name was added to the list of African nations—Tanzania—a name that unites Tanganyika, a former UN trust territory administered by Britain (Tanganyika won its independence in December, 1961), and the off-shore island of Zanzibar, formerly a British protectorate.

Tanganyika, with an area of 362,688 square miles and a population of 9,500,000, added another 1,020 square miles and about 300,000 people—two thirds of whom were Africans and the remainder Arabs, Italians, and a sprinkling of other Europeans—when Zanzibar became part of the new republic.

Swahili is spoken throughout the land, but English is the country's second language and the standard medium of instruction from the seventh grade up.

Tanzania has put a high priority on

In the hospital at Dar es Salaam, nurse Ethel Brown treats a patient who had been attacked and severely mangled by a lion.

Nurse Frances Hartery, center, assists in the operating room in the Mubinbili Hospital in Dar es Salaam. The surgeon is an Indian woman.

A new mother in the Mubinbili Hospital receives nursing instruction from Patsy Mason.

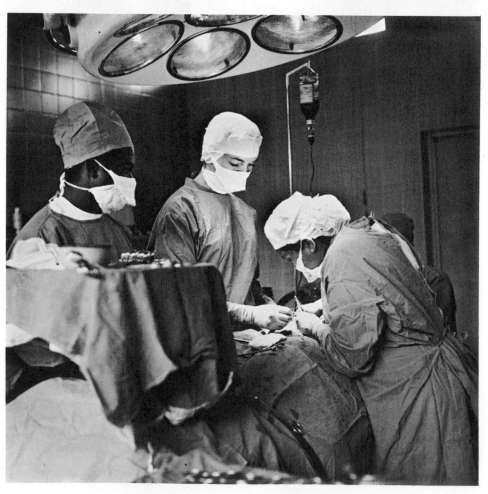

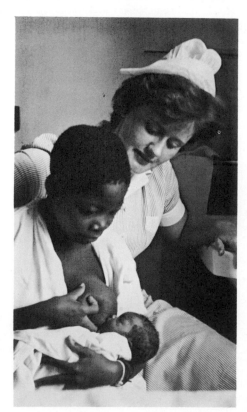

education in its first five-year plan. In his presentation of the plan to Parliament, President Julius K. Nyerere said, "One of the major long-term objectives of our planning is to be self-sufficient in trained manpower by 1980. This means a carefully planned expansion of education."

The Peace Corps was one of the first outside organizations to be recruited in this planning, and several large groups of Volunteers have been sent to the country since late 1961.

Among those who are serving there in a wide variety of fields are teachers, who make up the majority, nurses, engineers, surveyors, farm experts, architects, lawyers, and office secretaries. At the request of the government the entire program was more than tripled by December, 1964.

Among the nurses who worked in two of the nation's largest hospitals, the Mubinbili Hospital in Dar es Salaam, the capital, and the 414-bed Government Hospital in Tanga, were Ethel Brown

Teacher Henry Antkiewicz reviews his pupils before class in Mbozi. This custom, followed all over the country, dates from the days of German occupation (Tanganyika was a German colony from 1885 until 1916, known as German East Africa).

Working on a road project, engineer Arthur Young stops to talk to a Tanzanian tractor driver.

(Arlington, Va.), with twenty years of nursing experience behind her, Frances Hartery (Natick, Mass.), who was a nurse in the United States for seven years before joining the Peace Corps, and Patsy Mason (East Hampton, Mass.).

Deep inside the country, enduring the rigors of climate and terrain (Tanzania is a hot, humid country with two monsoon seasons that bring heavy rains), teachers like Vernon Richey (Charleston, Ill.), Leonard Levitt (Cedarhurst, N. Y.), Henry Antkiewicz (Hamtramck, Mich.), Patricia Pleasix (Darien, Conn.), and George Fries (Fresno, Calif.) were help-

Surveyor Jerry Parson, right, shows a Tanzanian trainee the proper technique for using the transit.

Below left, deep inside the Tanzanian bush country, Dick Van Loenen, a geologist, works with his crew on a steep rocky outcrop.

Below, a teacher of English, George Fries, explains a fine point of grammar to one of his students. His wife, Lita, taught in the same school in Mwanza, on the south shore of Lake Victoria.

ing to bring about a new era in education.

Among the engineers, geologists, and surveyors were Arthur Young (Schwenksville, Pa.), Matthew Wright (Kane, Pa.), Jerry Parson (Albany, N. Y.), and Dick Van Loenen (Bogue, Kan.).

Early one morning in January, 1964, an incident that could have seriously disrupted Peace Corps activity in Tanzania was narrowly averted. An army mutiny, confined to Dar es Salaam and several remote outposts, erupted. It was put down within three days. But before it was over, the lives of three Peace Corps nurses and

Patricia Pleasix gives a young Tanzanian an outdoor lesson in art. She and her husband, Alex, taught at the Nzovwe Middle School outside Mbeya, in southern Tanzania.

Wagogo children watch as Geologist Matthew Wright tries to play the zeze, a primitive violin. Wright worked for the government's Geological Survey Division, which prepared a geological map of the entire country. Wright and the other geologists—Volunteers and Tanzanians—lived under canvas deep in the bush and moved camp about every two or three weeks.

Speaking Swahili, Leonard Levitt chats with a Tanzanian woman outside her thatched hut in the southern town of Tukuyu. Levitt taught at the Mpuguso Upper Primary School there.

Vernon Richey and his students harvest their cotton crop, which will be sold to benefit the school in Mwanza. Income from cotton and other crops make the school almost entirely self-supporting. In addition to teaching, Vernon initiated a program of eye tests and arranged for needy students to be provided with glasses.

two teachers had been threatened. In Tabora, where the Volunteers were stationed, mutineers went out in search of "Europeans." When the soldiers went to the school, an African teacher hid the Peace Corps teachers in a closet in the principal's office until they left. Later, the mutineers appeared at the town's hospital and harassed the Peace Corps nurses there by firing shots over their heads. But the whole community quickly closed ranks to protect the Volunteers and, fortunately, no one was hurt.

Togo

From 1946 to 1960 a French-administered UN trusteeship in West Africa, the new Republic of Togo is a narrow, 330-mile-long ribbon of tropical countryside, pressed between Ghana and Dahomey, that runs north from its south-facing coast line. Its shore consists of thirty-five miles of white sand unbroken by any harbor. One enters Togo overland, via neighboring Ghana.

In 1962 Volunteer Michael Ruggiero (Peabody, Mass.), a fishing expert, went to Anécho, a small fishing community, with a team of eight fishermen he had selected in the United States. Within eight months the team had dwindled to five. Half of the promised equipment never arrived. And although Ruggiero worked hard and with imagination, the fishing catch of Anécho was not substantially increased.

On the other hand, Jackie Theriot (St. Martinville, La.) and Keith Keller (Marblehead, Mass.), whom Ruggiero had sent inland to set up fishpond farms and to stock streams, met with great success. But they were worried that their breeding stations would be destroyed through indifference and ignorance after they left.

Peter Lefcourt, a teacher from Flushing, New York, plays Aware, a game played with beans, in front of the village store in Woame.

Lefcourt teaching in a secondary school in Woame.

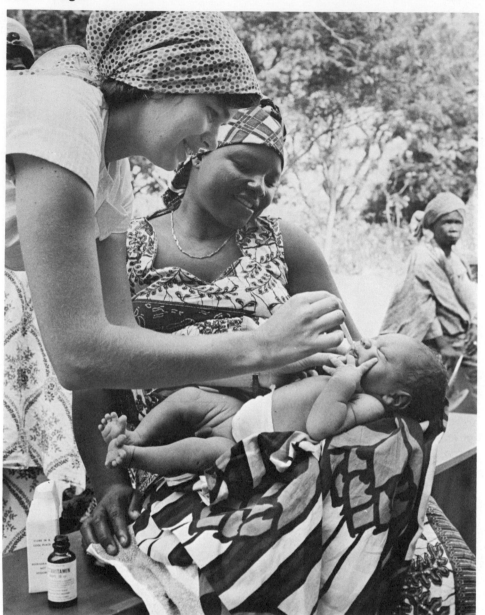

Left, nurse Ann Moore (West Alexandria, Ohio) gives vitamins to a baby at a clinic in Sokodé, a town about two hundred miles inland. Women patients gave her the scarf she is wearing.

Below, Peter Lefcourt chats with village children on their way to fetch fresh water.

Right, Michael Ruggiero, left center, George Toneatti (Gloucester, Mass.), with cap, and Vito Blonda (Ipswich, Mass.) help launch the large dugout in which they taught fishing techniques. Below, Ruggiero, one hundred miles off the coast of Anécho, offers instruction in tub trawling. This method employs a long line coiled in a tub, with hooks laid over the rim to prevent tangling. The lines are let out with a buoy at each end, strung out for about a half mile, one hundred hooks to the line.

Difficult problems were encountered and to some extent were left unsolved by teachers who went to Togo. Wrote one:

"You teach in a French system, subject to the Ministre National de l'Education, sometimes with French colleagues and a French school director. The system of discipline is Victorian. Kids are expected to sit in neat little rows and raise their hands if they have questions. Nobody is expected to talk out of turn, and nobody is expected to do anything, in fact, but listen to the teacher, respond to everything he says, and stand when the teacher enters or leaves a class. Above all, students: KEEP QUIET! Well, try to see that young Africans, used to sitting around the village fire at night, used to talking whether anyone listens or not—just try to see if they'll do that. They won't!"

Photo Credits

TRAINING: Paul Conklin. Clemens Kalischer, page 8.

BOLIVIA: Paul Conklin.

PERU: Paul Conklin.

CHILE: Paul Conklin.

ECUADOR: Paul Conklin.

VENEZUELA: Paul Conklin. Phillip D. Hardberger, page 46 (top).

BRAZIL: Paul Conklin.

EL SALVADOR: Paul Conklin.

DOMINICAN REPUBLIC: Paul Conklin.

BRITISH HONDURAS: Paul Conklin.

COLOMBIA: Ray Witlin (Black Star).

CYPRUS: Paul Conklin.

TURKEY: Paul Conklin. James Walls, page 78 (top).

AFGHANISTAN: Paul Conklin.

PAKISTAN: Paul Conklin.

NEPAL: Paul Conklin.

THAILAND: Thomas S. Plaut. Rowland Scherman, pages 111 (bottom) and 113 (middle).

MALAYSIA: Thomas S. Plaut. Rowland Scherman, page 118 (bottom).

TUNISIA: Paul Conklin.

MOROCCO: Paul Conklin.

GUINEA: Paul Conklin.

GHANA: John Moss (Black Star). John and Bini Moss (Black Star), page 136 (top).

ETHIOPIA: Phillip D. Hardberger. Rowland Scherman, page 138 (bottom).

CAMEROON: Morton R. Engelberg.

LIBERIA: John Moss (Black Star).

SIERRA LEONE: Paul Conklin.

NIGERIA: Morton R. Engelberg. Rowland Scherman, pages 148 (bottom) and 150 (bottom); Wide World, page 149 (bottom right).

TANZANIA: Phillip D. Hardberger. John Moss (Black Star), pages 153 (bottom) and 154 (top); John and Bini Moss (Black Star), pages 154 (bottom left) and 155 (bottom).

TOGO: Rowland Scherman.

Photograph of John F. Kennedy and Sargent Shriver by Rowland Scherman.

Composition by Clarke & Way in English Monotype Bembo and Univers.

Designed by David J. Way and Katherine Hahn.

Printed by New York Lithographing Corporation.

Bound by American Book–Stratford Press Incorporated.

THE PEACE CORPS